bull·shit
[b*oo*'l-shit]

bull·shit

[b*oo*'l-shit]

a lexicon

Mark Peters

Illustrated by Drew Dernavich

 Three Rivers Press / New York

Library of Congress Cataloging-in-Publication Data
Peters, Mark, 1972–
Bullshit : a lexicon / Mark Peters.
1. Truthfulness and falsehood—Humor.   2. Nonsense—
Humor.   3. English language—United States—Jargon—
Humor.   I. Title.
PN6231.T74P48 2015
427—dc23   2015014976

ISBN 978-1-101-90453-4
eBook ISBN 978-1-101-90454-1

Printed in the United States of America

Book design by Ellen Cipriano
Illustrations by Drew Dernavich
Cover design by Michael Morris

10 9 8 7 6 5 4 3 2 1

First Edition

To my parents, Edward and Janet,
who have had to deal with a lot of bullshit

Bullshit is everywhere.

—Jon Stewart

bull·shit

[bʊʊ'l-shit]

Introduction

Like you, I hate bullshit. But I kind of love it too—at least the words for it.

Malarkey! Bunk! Mule fritters! Flubdub! Selling wolf tickets! All my eye and Betty Martin!

Who wouldn't love words like that? The lingo of bullshit is earthy, silly, bonkers, and fun. And (at the risk of mansplaining) it's a lot bigger than you think.

I've been writing about words for over ten years and in dozens of publications. I write about euphemisms, new words, slang, etc. But while writing about lexical this and linguistic that, I kept getting drawn to words for bullshit.

At first I didn't know the BS vocabulary went beyond well-known words such as *mumbo jumbo, balderdash, tommy-rot, rubbish,* and *crapola.* But then I would stumble upon a word like *skimble-skamble:* a rare term used by Shakespeare that can mean bullshit. I'd notice that *flummery* has wild variations like *flummadiddle*. I'd learn a great idiom like the British *all gas and gaiters*. Sometimes a BS word would enter my life more dramatically: I was lucky enough to be at the American Dialect Society meeting that voted *truthiness* 2005's Word of the Year. Word by word, I noticed there were far more terms for bullshit than I had ever imagined. My own searches in the *Oxford English Dictionary*—and the generous assistance of dictionary editors such as Jonathon Green (*Green's Dictionary of Slang*) and Joan Hall (*Dictionary of American Regional English*)—confirmed it. BS is all over the English language, like horse apples on a country road.

This book explores that lexicon, giving a tour of more than two hundred words and phrases—well-known and obscure, filthy and euphemistic—that mean bullshit (or something with a very strong whiff of it). Along the way, you'll also find a few words for bullshitters and bullshitting.

So what is bullshit? In his great essay "On Bullshit," Harry Frankfurt distinguishes BS from lies. As Frankfurt explains, "The bullshitter is faking things. But this does not mean that he necessarily gets them wrong." For Frankfurt, lies and bullshit exist in parallel universes, independent of each other. The bullshitter is more of a poser than a liar.

But language is slippery, and we use the word *bullshit* for many things. There is a bullshit spectrum, which includes the following, in order of decreasing complexity:

scams

lies

gossip

empty boasts

sentimental crap

insignificant things

rubbish

gibberish

Words that apply to a specific type of bullshit tend to eventually get applied to other forms too. For example, *mumbo jumbo* was originally superstitious nonsense, but the word can now be used for virtually any type of bullshit. *Trumpery* still tends to be used most often for the insignificant type of bullshit, but it's sometimes used more broadly. *Treacle* refers to sentimental, phony bullshit, and it's stayed close to that meaning. Each BS word has its own range of meaning, but they're all linked—with *bullshit* at the center.

Just as certain types of soil are more conducive to farming and certain bars are more conducive to brawling, there are a few subject areas and word types that tend to produce bullshit words.

Animals

The barnyard has been very good to the bullshit lexicon. Of course, there's *bullshit* itself and all related words. Then there are the various horse terms: *horseshit, horsefeathers, horse apples, horse hockey, horsepucky,* etc. Words like *batshit*—which can mean bullshit or insanity—also live in the bullshit zoo.

Food and Drink

The bullshit lexicon is not limited to one end of the digestive journey: eating and drinking are also well represented. Such words include *balderdash* and *balductum,* which originally referred to drinks with a disgusting assortment of ingredients. This is the kind of bullshit you definitely don't want to swallow. Many BS terms have a similar "make you sick" origin. Other foods—such as *fudge, rhubarb,* and *spinach*—aren't as inedible but still ended up on the lexical shelf next to *twaddle* and *rot.*

Air

On a less solid and disgusting note, the very air we breathe is often associated with bullshit: specifically the hot air we expel when giving *guff* (originally a puff of wind). This idea animates words such as *airy-fairy* and *bloviator.* If an idea is as insubstantial as air, it's probably bullshit.

Politics

This prolific category includes *bunk,* which evolved from *bunkum* and the expression *speaking for Buncombe,* which involves politically motivated pandering. Terms such as *spin,* George Orwell's *newspeak,* and Stephen Colbert's *truthiness* are also mainly political.

Scams

Words such as *shenanigan, gammon,* and *flimflam* refer to the type of bullshit that involves hornswoggling people out of their money in some way. These words originally had to do with sweet deals involving something like bridges or snake oil. Today this type of bullshit is associated with fake Nigerian princes or Ponzi schemes.

Science Fiction

Science fiction often produces euphemisms and pseudo-obscenities, and that includes words for bullshit. Examples include *targ manure* from *Star Trek, felgercarb* from the original *Battlestar Galactica,* and *crapspackle* from *Futurama.*

There are also a few types of words that act as lightning rods for bullshit.

Reduplication

Reduplication is the process that creates words such as *dillydally, hocus-pocus,* and *night-night,* which represent the three most common types. You can repeat the word, changing only the vowel, as in *twittle-twattle*. You can change the initial consonant but keep the rest of the word, as in *helter-skelter*. Or you can repeat the whole word, as in *choo-choo*. Maybe because of the nonsensical sound, reduplication has been a bottomless well of BS words, including *mumbo jumbo, arkymalarkey, fiddle-faddle, jibber-jabber, yakety-yak,* and *flubdub*.

Words for Bullshitters

Besides *bullshit artist,* there are quite a few terms for someone who knows how to talk twaddle. These terms can sound scientific (*philosophunculist*), disgusting (*four-flusher*), or Irish (*gobshite*).

There are also idioms (*all mouth and no trousers, talk through one's hat*), euphemisms (*gentleman cow, meadow mayonnaise*), words that have spread rapidly on the Internet (*humblebrag, mansplaining*), academic terms (*casuistry, sophistry*), folksy terms (*belly wash, rannygazoo*), Cockney rhyming slang (*Niagara Falls, Jackson Pollocks*), borrowed words (*meshugas* from Yiddish, *quatsch* from German), and eponyms (*Barnum, Mickey Mouse*).

There's a lot of bullshit out there, and there's a lot of bullshit in here.

Even so, it would be utter horseshit to say this book is

complete. But I've included all of the most common words for bullshit and bullshitters, plus a ton of obscurities. Bullshit research is ongoing, so please drop me a line (@wordlust) if you have a bullshit word to share or just want to bullshit about bullshit.

abracadabra

Abracadabra is the kind of magical word you expect to hear when a dude in a top hat is pulling a rabbit out of another hat, sawing a woman in half, or making the Statue of Liberty disappear.

But *abracadabra* also means bullshit.

The word originally had a woo-woo meaning not far from its eventual magical sense: It referred to spells and charms for healing. In fact, the word was used not only in speech; it was written on a piece of paper, with a letter removed in each line, like this:

abracadabra
abracadabr
abracadab
abracada
abracad
abraca
abrac
abra
abr
ab
a

The paper was then folded up and inserted into an amulet. Somehow, this was thought to help cure lupus or something, perhaps with the help of herbs and incantations.

From such medical hoodwinks, *abracadabra* also came to be used by professional magicians, which is mainly how we know the word today. But it also moved to the lexicon of general nonsense.

For example, this 1867 use from *Biblical Repertory:* "Swedenborg's writings, as a whole, are unintelligible—abracadabra—to any other." Another strong takedown of written bullshit appeared in a 1934 letter by poet Dylan Thomas: "Piece One is remarkable for the number of entirely meaningless & affected words you have managed to drag in. 'Dulcimer,' 'Drumdeep,' 'Cohorts,' & 'Silken Shadowy Girls.' All the damned abracadabra of the Poet's Corner, and as gutless as a filleted herring."

Ouch. Filleted herring = mucho malarkey.

ackamarackus

Watch out for *the old ackamarackus.* The formula *the old _____* is common in expressions for swindles and scams. If someone gave you the old okey-doke or the old flimflam, you got hustled. But the old ackamarackus is not just deceptive—it's a big, showy production. With syllables to spare, *ackamarackus* is the Broadway musical of BS words.

The *Oxford English Dictionary* defines this rhyming word

as "Something regarded as pretentious nonsense; something intended to deceive; humbug." A 1954 use in a review from London's *Sunday Times* demonstrates the kind of showy, flamboyant stuff associated with the word: "The story is about an American circus in Germany, a spiv [petty criminal] who picks up a German floozie, a high diver who marries her, and a dumb giant who brings her wayside flowers." This colorful, chaotic combo of characters was summed up by writer Dawn Powell: "In fact, it is the old circus ackamarackus."

If you have something simple and/or honest to present, you don't need a lot of bells and whistles, and you certainly don't need the major-league ballyhoo that is an ackamarackus.

airy-fairy

This term originally had to do with real fairies—well, with the real idea of a fairy. The first known uses, from the mid-1800s, all have to do with magical, ethereal, or light stuff, such as dresses and music. In the 1800s *airy-fairy* also gravitated toward bullshit, probably because the fanciful world of fairies was far removed from the practical business of getting a damn job, you lazy bums.

By 1920 you could see examples like D. H. Lawrence's description in *Lost Girl* of a character with "an airy-fairy kind of knowledge of the whole affair." That kind of expertise is anything but airtight.

all gas and gaiters

It's fitting that a phrase for nonsense seems to have originated as nonsense: terms linked by alliteration and little else.

As Michael Quinion of *World Wide Words* notes, *all gas and gaiters* first appears in Charles Dickens' *Nicholas Nickleby* and is used by a character who is, to use a technical term, bonkers. Even so, the expression had a positive vibe, which informed its early use for any satisfactory or swell state of affairs: "I see her now; I see her now! My love, my life, my bride, my peerless beauty. She is come at last—at last—and all is gas and gaiters!" The logic was unclear, but the meaning was not: When all is gas and gaiters, everything's cool, fine, dandy, awesome, groovy, etc.

As so often happens with seemingly incomprehensible terms, people tried to make sense of *all gas and gaiters*— mainly through interpreting the gaiters, which are protec-

tive cloth coverings for the legs. As slang expert Jonathon Green notes, the term conjures the "image of a pompous, sermonizing (and be-gaitered) bishop." Since such men of the cloth also tend to be gasbags, an illogical, random term gained a new meaning and a path to the lexicon of bullshit. If you're all gas and gaiters, you're minimum substance with maximum hot air.

By 1923 the term's shift to hot air and hokum was complete. In 1932 George Bernard Shaw used the idiom with characteristic wit, referring to a poem by Percy Bysshe Shelley as "literary gas and gaiters."

All Gas and Gaiters was also the name of a 1960s British sitcom. That title pretty much meant *All Bullshit*.

all mouth and no trousers

If you're all gas and gaiters, you're alliteratively full of it. Likewise, if you're all mouth and no trousers, you're good at blabbing but not so good at action. You don't back up your words, you noxious ninnyhammer.

This idiom is a good example of language evolution. The original version was *all mouth and trousers*. That use suggested a horny fellow, trying every pickup line in the book and thinking with his trouser region. A use in L. P. Hartley's 1961 short story collection *Two for the River* slyly plays on this meaning: "It's not a bad life. Most men are all mouth and trousers—well, I like the trousers best, if you know what I mean."

I think I do.

Eventually the idiom started taking on the negative form *all mouth and no trousers,* possibly influenced by *all talk and no action.* The meaning also shifted—away from lasciviousness to any kind of empty words.

It's best not to take this expression to heart. If you meet someone who's literally all mouth and no trousers, call the police.

all my eye and Betty Martin

This satisfying exclamation—which Agatha Christie enjoyed and used often—has many close relatives. Saying "My eye!" is a way of saying "That's bullshit!" or "Oh, come on!" You can also say "My foot!" or "My ass!" if your exclamatory anatomical preferences are less ocular.

The phrase *all my eye* also means nonsense. Though this is a mostly dated expression going back to the late 1700s, it still turns up once in a while, as in this 2012 use in the *Irish Times:* "So attractive as it is, that explanation may itself be all my eye." Overattractive, neat explanations of anything do tend to be pure poppycock.

Which brings us to the more dramatic version of this expression: *All my eye and Betty Martin!* Translation: "That is such a huge load of crap I need a two-part exclamation to dismiss it!"

Who was Betty Martin? No one knows for sure. Some think the name was part of a lost Latin prayer, but since the prayer is lost, who knows? Others think it was a piece of nautical equipment. Maybe she was just a London woman who liked to say "All my eye!" a lot. We may never know the true origin, but if you ever meet a Betty Martin, congratulate her on being part of bullshit history.

applesauce

It's obvious why some words become synonyms for bullshit. Horseshit and rubbish aren't highly valued, to say the least.

But *applesauce*? That origin isn't so clear. Maybe this term was influenced by *horse apples,* a euphemism for horseshit. Or maybe applesauce tasted like pure crap to someone, because this has been a synonym for nonsense since at least the 1920s. Often it means lies or flattery, as in this example from Ring Lardner Jr.'s *The Love Nest and Other Stories:* "I wasn't born yesterday and I know apple sauce when I hear it and I bet you've told that to fifty girls."

The word can also be used a simple dismissal of something. If a friend said, "I heard you hate nachos," you could reply, "Applesauce!" as a firm denial. Then you could tell your friend to make up for the insult by buying you nachos.

babble

These days there are two main types of babble: the prelanguage vocalizations of a baby and the postlanguage bullshit of an adult. But the word *babble* has had a gaggle of meanings over the years, and many are related to too much blah-blah.

The very first meanings, found in the 1200s, refer to excess chatter, so this word was always close to meaning bullshit. By the 1500s that meaning had evolved to include a type of blabbing: giving away secret info unintentionally or incautiously.

Meanwhile, the word took a detour to the animal kingdom as a word for birdsong, as shown in this 1823 use by Isaac D'Israeli in *Knickerbocker* magazine: "When a nest of swallows began to babble he hushed them." Apparently, babbling birds can be as unwelcome as yammering dudes. A use from over a hundred years later, in Jacob Neusner's *The Idea of Purity in Ancient Judaism,* shows the connection between bird and human babble: "Just as birds chirp, or babble, so did the common gossip." Elsewhere on the food chain, a hound was said to babble if he barked wildly, presumably in a way that didn't help with hunting.

Babble was such a successful word for various types of BS, it also became a suffix.

The children of *babble* include *ecobabble, econobabble, Eurobabble, Franco-babble,* and *technobabble*. But the most successful such word might be *psychobabble,* which has been around since the mid-1970s, meaning any lingo or ideas, especially technical or pretentious, from the then-booming world of popular psychology. If anyone is talking about releasing their inner child, wrestling with their inner demons, feeling their feelings, having their needs met, or getting in touch with—well, anything—psychobabble is on the march.

Inane self-help sayings also fit under the umbrella of psychobabble. You know the ones: those "inspiring" nuggets of nothingness your worst Facebook friends tend to post. "Dance like no one is watching." "Everything happens for a reason." "No one can hurt you without your permission."

On Twitter, TV personality Damien Fahey summed up such psychobabble well: "It's never your super successful friends posting the inspirational quotes."

baboonery

Poor baboons. Though they are close relatives of humans, their name has long been used in insulting terms that sometimes fall on the bullshit spectrum.

In the 1600s the term *baboonery* had a straightforward

meaning: a colony of baboons. The word then spread to rubbishy art, wild stupidity, and general foolishness.

A 2014 comment on an article from *Science* magazine shows the term isn't extinct: "Claiming a fixed field would be relative solely to the Earth's orbit is not only wrong in more ways than one. . . . It is complete baboonery."

Baboons are noble beasts, but they have never done well at astronomy.

baked wind

This surprisingly nonflatulent term refers to the kind of breath that has a high temperature and a higher BS quotient: hot air.

In his 1910 collection *Love Sonnets of a Hoodlum,* Wallace Irwin offers a damning description of a type of person who is "smooth as eels and slick as soap. A baked-wind expert." In other words, a smooth operator and bullshit artist.

Conservative humorist P. J. O'Rourke used this term in his 1996 book *The Enemies List,* referring to "members and cohorts of the Clinton administration, those simps and ninnies, lava-lamp liberals and condo pinks, spoiled twerps, wiffenpoofs, ratchet-jawed purveyors of monkey doodle and baked wind."

It's no wonder a skilled writer like O'Rourke digs this term (along with the equally charming *monkey doodle* and *wiffenpoof*). *Hot air* is boring white bread compared to the vibrant, multigrain wonders of *baked wind.*

balderdash

Balderdash was originally an ill-advised mixture of beverages, such as beer with wine or beer with milk. If you're gagging at the thought, you understand the original meaning of *balderdash,* which was used throughout the 1600s by frustrated bar patrons.

Then, in the second half of the seventeenth century, the word took a turn: It began to apply to words that went together as badly as milk and beer. Nonsense, tripe, and jibber-jabber became balderdash.

A quotation from Thomas Babington Macaulay's 1849 book *The History of England from the Accession of James II* captures the meaning of the word: "I am almost ashamed to quote such nauseous balderdash."

So should we all be, Thomas Babington. So should we all.

balductum

Because it has a Latin ring to it, this word sounds quite serious. It would be scary coming out of a doctor's mouth. However, it thankfully does not name a rare medical condition.

Balductum sounds like a mixture of *balderdash* and *bunkum,* though it has no direct relationship to either word—but it is close in meaning to *balderdash.* This fifteenth-century term is another word for a posset, which is a hot drink involving curdled milk and booze, such as ale or wine. Yum?

In the 1500s this word for such swill came to mean bullshit, especially a type of bullshit that involves mismatched stuff thrown together. In 1593 Gabriel Harvey used the term in *Pierces Supererogation; or, A New Prayse of the Old Asse,* mocking "the stalest dudgen, or absurdest balductum, that they, or their mates can inuent [*sic*]." Harvey lambasted the dullest clichés or most preposterous fiddle-faddle that anyone could pull out of their ass.

Just like the original drink, figurative balductum sounded about as appealing as a combo of orange juice, chicken-wing sauce, and toothpaste.

balls, bollocks

These two words can be found in the exclamatory section of the bullshit menu. Both can mean roughly "Damn!" or "Shit!" but they're also frequently used to call bullshit.

The word *balls* came before and inspired *bollocks,* but they share the same unfortunate meanings: testicles and nonsense.

Back in 1915, poet Ezra Pound used the older term in a letter to Irish writer James Joyce: "I am so damn sick of energetic stupidity. The 'strong' work . . . balls!" A 2000 sentence recorded by word guy Jonathon Green should amuse anyone skeptical of graduate school: "You think you need a huge fucking brain to get a PhD? Balls."

If you want to be slightly more verbose—and much more British—use *bollocks,* as George Orwell did in 1936 when he discussed a publishing delay caused by "all that bollux about libel." Another notable writer, Philip Larkin, used the word self-deprecatingly in 1940: "I suppose my writing is terrible. Sod & ballocks, anyway."

So why are these words for nonsense? Are testicles that bad? Jonathon Green suggests a connection stemming from an early use of *bollocks* to refer to a parson. Green wonders if the term shifted to nonsense "on the premise that sermonizing is, de facto, nonsense." Heaven forbid the thought.

Green's theory is plausible but not definitive. It's probably at least half balls.

baloney, phony baloney, phonus balonus

Baloney is one of the most common words for bullshit, and as with so many other words, its origin isn't known. But there are theories.

We do know the Italian town of Bologna produced Bologna sausage. Given the inherently suspect nature of sausage, it's assumed *Bologna* became *baloney,* with bullshitty meat becoming, simply, bullshit.

Unfortunately, there isn't any actual evidence that this is the origin of *baloney* as a word for bullshit. The truth is, we don't know where *baloney* came from, though we know it started being used in the 1920s (along with variant spelling *boloney*). This 1935 use from a *Discovery* magazine article about the growing role of psychiatry gives a sense of the meaning, discussing the idea "that much of modern psychiatry is 'hooey' and 'baloney.'" Like *malarkey* and *horseshit,* *baloney* can mean just about any type of bullshit.

People like using *baloney* so much that the term has spawned a few variations. Not long after the appearance of *baloney, phony baloney* appeared. And from there it was only one more step to *phonus balonus:* a word for fraud or trickery that has a pseudo-Latin sound.

Baloney. Phony baloney. Phonus balonus. Like animals, words evolve. (Unless you think evolution is bullshit.)

ballyhoo

Ballyhoo started popping up in the early 1900s. A ballyhoo was originally a pitchman's spiel, exhorting people to come see the carnival. As in today's insufferable marketing campaigns, there wasn't a high standard for honesty or restraint. This use from *Europe Revised* by Irvin Shrewsbury Cobb in 1914 gives a sense of loud, enthusiastic huckstering: "a live, little park full of sideshow tents sheltering mildly amusing, faked-up attractions, with painted banners flapping in the air and barkers spieling before the entrances and all the ballyhoos going at full blast."

From there it was a short journey to general bullshit, but this word still applies mostly to bullshit that raises a fuss of some sort. Ballyhoo is loud and obnoxious, as opposed to the complex bullshit of sophistry or the trifling bullshit of trumpery.

Let's say someone said, of the latest *Breaking Bad* or *The Wire* type show: "Oh my God, you have to watch this TV show: It is the best TV show in the history of this universe or any other!" An appropriate response would be: "Take the ballyhoo down a notch."

banana oil, bananas

The banana is the craziest fruit. But *bananas*—and *banana oil*—can also mean bullshit.

Besides the close relationship between bullshit and craziness, this term is inspired by amyl acetate solution—which is nicknamed *banana liquid* or *banana oil* for its smell and is used in various foods and medicines.

English writer and humorist P. G. Wodehouse used this term in his 1960 novel *Jeeves in the Offing,* mentioning "the sort of banana oil that passes between statesmen at conferences conducted in an atmosphere of the utmost cordiality before they tear their whiskers off and get down to cases." Apparently, it was the smoothness of banana oil that led to its being used as a term for flattery and other smooth talk. If you didn't have the relevant facts or a strong argument, you had to resort to banana oil. Slippery liquids go well with slippery words.

You can also shout "Bananas!" if "Hogwash!" and "Bunk!" have gotten tiresome. F. Scott Fitzgerald used that sense of the word in 1940's *Pat Hobby Stories,* as the title character responded to some hurtful accusations with "Aw, bananas." That response was equivalent to "Come on, man. That's not true."

Barnum

This obscure, out-of-fashion term, which originated in the 1800s, came from Phineas Taylor Barnum of the Barnum & Bailey Circus. Since such shows were showy as hell, the name *Barnum* came to stand for nonsense that was particularly high on hype and low on substance. Often this meant a type of hoax or scam, as alluded to in this use by George Douglas Brewerton in his 1856 book *The War in Kansas:* "He believed the whole affair to be a 'Barnum'—alias humbug, of the most unmitigated kind." James Joyce used the term in 1914's *Stephen Hero:* "It's absurd: it's Barnum." In other words, "It's ridiculous; it's rot."

If something is Barnum, it's not what it appears to be, especially if it appears to be spectacular. This flashy sort of bullshit can even extend to seemingly low-key researchers, as seen in a *Daily Express* example from 1937: "There is a touch of Barnum about scientists which sets them whooping when any one of them has found something new." I'd say most Facebook friends also have a little Barnum, given the fanfare and hoopla they attach to their children and meals.

batshit

These days, *batshit* is a pretty common slang word for crazy. You can say someone is batshit, batshit crazy, or batshit insane. They can also descend into batshit madness or another guano-related variation.

However, before *batshit* went batty, it was simply bullshit. The very earliest known uses, which go back to 1950, are far closer to horseshit than to nuttiness.

The crazy sense picked up in the 1970s, but this use from Dean Koontz's 1985 novel *Door to December* shows the

BS sense never entirely faded: "Why would men of science associate with a purveyor of bat shit and bunkum?"

Why, indeed? Purveyors of alliterative bullshit should never be trusted.

bavardage

This rare nineteenth-century word for idle chitchat has a surprising amount of gravitas, possibly due to its repeated low sounds and echoes of *bastard* and *garbage.* It would likely feel pretty great to stand up in the middle of a staff meeting or family dinner and shout, "Bavardage!"

The roots of this word are French and related to words for chattering, talkativeness, and saliva/drivel, so its lexical brethren are soaked in bullshit. An 1882 example from the *Quarterly Review* describes a common response to BS: "They were browbeat, contradicted, told to cease their bavardage." Basically, they were told to shut up and cut the crapola.

This word is rare in English these days, but it's pretty common among the French—those lucky, *bavardage*-hoarding bastards.

beans

Poor beans. Lexically they don't mean shit, but they do mean bullshit.

If you don't know beans, you don't know anything. You can also say you don't care beans for something. A common expression for near-diddly-squat is "a hill of beans." That expression is lovingly tweaked in the comedy classic *The Naked Gun,* when Leslie Nielsen's Frank Drebin says to his gun-toting, mind-controlled paramour—we've all been there—"It's a topsy-turvy world, and maybe the problems of two people don't amount to a hill of beans. But this is our hill. And these are our beans!"

All those negative or minimizing meanings made *beans* a perfect word for nonsense. It doesn't hurt that it starts with the same letter as *balls* and *bollocks* and sometimes has the same testicular meaning.

Most often *beans* means nonsense in the gaseous expression "full of beans." If you're full of beans, you are not full of logic, facts, common sense, or anything interesting. You're just full of it.

belcher

No one appreciates a belcher, with a few exceptions. Some gifted individuals can say the entire alphabet in one lengthy burp: Such virtuosos of the belch are like legendary fartiste Joseph Pujol, who turned his hiney into a musical instrument, wowing crowds in nineteenth-century France.

Gross yet impressive bodily control aside, the word *belcher* also means a spewer of nonsense. A 1914 use recorded by Jonathon Green tellingly mentions "Belchers and Boshers." When you're lumped with boshers, you're in a high-BS crowd—as if the smelly, gaseous nature of belching weren't clue enough.

Another sense of this term has been around since the early twentieth century and is also related to bullshit, according to secretive types: an informant. A 1951 use in the *New Yorker* shows this sense of the word in verb form: "I feel good that I didn't belch on a pal, because that's the code I was raised on." Belching on a pal, literally or figuratively, is never welcome. The term can also mean someone who complains a lot or just won't shut up in general.

A belch is full of hot air and stinks. That makes it the perfect metaphor for going on about your children, complaining about the weather, testifying in court, or just spouting a bunch of bilge.

belly wash

Depending on where you live, you might use the term *soda* or *pop* for carbonated sugar drinks. Or you might say *belly wash*.

This has been a term for a soft drink since the early 1900s. A 1964 article from the *Journal of American Folklore* mentions that a Pennsylvania pop-bottling plant was referred to as the "belly-wash factory." Such uses led *belly wash* to also be used for weak alcohol—stuff that would get you about as drunk as a root beer or ginger ale.

And from there it became a term for nonsense, much

like the far more popular *hogwash*. *Belly wash* isn't common, but it shows up from time to time. Here it is in a 2004 message-board post about lowering the voting age: "This is the biggest bunch of belly wash." Given the toxic composition of soft drinks and the timeless tragedy of weak liquor, *belly wash* has a perfect bullshit pedigree.

Ben Cartwright

Who was Ben Cartwright and what did he do to become a synonym for bullshit?

Was he a corrupt politician? A career criminal? A bridge salesman? Maybe he was a celebrity like Gwyneth Paltrow who used a lot of mumbo-jumbo terms like *conscious uncoupling*.

Nah. Ben Cartwright was just a fictional character whose name had an unfortunate rhyme.

Ben Cartwright was a character on the classic American TV show *Bonanza*, which ran from 1959 to 1973. Cartwright, played by Lorne Greene, was a cattle rancher and patriarch of the Cartwright family. He was probably less full of shit than other characters on the show, but his last name rhymed with the British *shite*. For British viewers of this American show, this was a perfect opening for Cockney rhyming slang, in which *apples and pears* means *stairs* and *Jack Jones* means *alone*. So Ben Cartwright became *shite*, besmirching this famous cowpoke's name with bullshit.

This term is rare, but it does pop up on a 2002 pornographic—er, erotic-story website: "I can't believe my king lears: what a pile of ben cartwright!"

Sorry, Ben (and Lorne). Rhyming slang is cruel.

bilge

Bullshit terms can pop up anywhere: on land, in the sky—even at sea.

Since the 1500s *bilge* has referred to a part of a ship, specifically the bottom of the hull. In the 1800s *bilge* started to refer to the filth and grime that collected on that part of a ship. This 1856 quotation from poet Ralph Waldo Emerson says it all: "Nobody likes to be treated ignominiously, upset, shoved against the side of the house, rolled over, suffocated with bilge, mephitis, and stewing oil." Bilge is grody to the max.

That's probably why by the 1900s *bilge* had gone metaphorical, and the metaphor included bullshit. A 1954 use in *Jeeves and the Feudal Spirit* by P. G. Wodehouse is appropriately insulting: "She wrote this novel and it was well received by the intelligentsia, who notoriously enjoy the most frightful bilge."

Bilge's journey from the filth of a ship to the pretensions of the intelligentsia is a good example of the versatility of BS words and their ability to migrate from other lexicons.

It's also a perfect BS word to use on September 19: Talk Like a Pirate Day.

bird turd, birdseed

Bird turd, at once pleasant due to the rhyme and gross due to the meaning, has been used in several ways that indicate BS or nonsense. A few uses recorded in *Green's Dictionary of Slang* suggest worlds of possibility beyond what some pigeon left on your windshield: bullshit and bullshitting.

In *The Naked and the Dead* Norman Mailer writes, "You ain't just a bird-turding, Jack." That can pretty easily be translated as "You're not shitting me." The term is often used in the negative sense: People are praised for not bird-turding more often than they're condemned for bird-turding. If only we gave the same positive reinforcement to actual birds.

What goes into a bird can also refer to bullshit: specifically, birdseed. In "Guns at Cyrano's" Raymond Chandler writes, "I've been getting threats. Maybe it's a lot of bird-seed." In *On the Waterfront* Terry Malloy asks a suspiciously inquisitive dude: "O.K. O.K. Without the bird seed. What do you want?" This was a clever way of saying: "Get to the point and cut the crap."

Ashes to ashes, birdseed to bird turds: It's all bullshit.

blah blah blah

Imagine the sound of someone droning on and on, like the incomprehensible teacher's voice in *Peanuts* specials. Sounds a little like *blah blah blah,* doesn't it?

The term apparently originated as an imitation of what too much talking, especially talking without a point, sounds like. A classic case of *blah* can be seen in this 1921 use from *Collier's:* "Then a special announcer began a long debate with himself which was mostly blah blah." How could it not be? When someone delivers a monologue, it's usually heavy on blah.

This word can also be used as a verb, whether in the *blah* or *blah-blah* form. You can blah about baseball, and I can blah-blah about basketball. In 1945 George Orwell used the term in his *Chicago Tribune* column about another sport: "Instead of blah-blahing about the clean, healthy rivalry of the football field and the great part played by the Olympic Games in bringing the nations together, it is more useful to inquire how and why this modern cult of sport arose."

If only today's blowhards on ESPN and other channels took those words to heart.

blandander

This rhyming word has slipped through the cracks of English, but not for lack of personality.

Arising from an Irish word for flattery, *blandander* continued this meaning in English in the late 1800s as a word for cajoling and sugarcoating. A use by versatile author George Bernard Shaw in 1896 refers to "a coaxing, blandandhering sort of liar."

Coaxing reinforces the meaning well. People who blandander are nagging, wheedling folks who lay it on thick.

This word hasn't had quite the success of its close relatives *blander* and *blandishment,* but it has a winning sound and undeniable usefulness. It's a shame few people take the time to blandander on behalf of *blandander.* We could use an alternative to *flatter.*

blarney

Blarney, as in the Blarney Stone, is bullshit: specifically, flattery and other manipulative chatter.

The origin of the term has to do with the legend of the Blarney Stone. As the story goes, the stone is located in a difficult-to-reach part of the village of Blarney. If you kiss the stone, you receive the gift of irresistible gab. The Blarney Stone is a bullshit enhancer.

Blarney as BS is first found in the late 1700s and has been used ever since in sentences like this 1819 one from George Crabbe's *Tales of the Hall:* "Bah!—bother!—blarney!—What is this about?" Writer D. H. Lawrence used it well, in an extremely pragmatic sentence from 1925: "Perfect love, I suppose, means that a married man and woman never contradict one another. . . . What blarney!"

With a hint of *malarkey* and a close resemblance to *baloney, blarney* brings the bunk of the Irish to the BS lexicon.

blather, blither

Blather comes from a Norse word for nonsense, and it has had several forms: *blather, blether,* and *blither. Blether* is oldest and started appearing in English in the 1500s. They all add up to a lot of yada yada.

Like *yap, blab,* and *blah,* these words tend to be used, in noun or verb form, for a flood of words and a drought of sense. If you enjoy what you're hearing in any way, it's not blather. If you're yearning for the speaker to shut the hell up, it is. Blathering is a real-life soliloquy with none of the entertainment value.

Blithering often appears in the expression "blithering idiot." Statistically, I'm not sure if idiots really do blither more often than morons or dum-dums. Further research is needed.

bloviate

This word and its variations are part of the hot-air section of the periodic table of bullshit. You can hear the word *blow* in *bloviate,* which is done by blowhards.

U.S. president Warren Harding apparently enjoyed using this word, and he often gets credit for inventing it. Ben Zimmer—the Indiana Jones of lexicography—dug up what might be the oldest direct use of the word by Harding, from the *Columbus (Georgia) Daily Enquirer* in 1920. The article reads:

> President-elect W.G. Harding in his address to the Elks here last week, coined a new word, which, insofar as can be determined, has never before been used. In describing the kind of person an Elk is, the Senator is quoted as saying: "An Elk is a person, who, when he does a good deed, keeps the knowledge thereof in his own breast and does not 'bloviate.'"

In reality, the term is older, going back to at least the mid-1800s. Many uses are from Harding's native state of Ohio, so it seems Harding simply brought a local term to the world stage.

This is a perfect term for politics in any era, as it brings to mind the bombastic, self-important, speechifying blather of politicians. *Bloviators*—to use another variation—aren't just full of hot air: They're full of a metric buttload of hot air, which you can call *bloviation*.

bosh

There is something to be said for one-syllable words. Look at how many exclamations and obscenities are one syllable: Damn! Shit! Fuck! Ow! Hey! Yikes! Sometimes you just don't have the time or patience for a second syllable.

Bosh is a word for nonsense that fits that pattern, and it is quite satisfying—at least if you're British—to exclaim when faced with a bunch of bollocks. While you can use the word as a noun by saying something is "total bosh" or "a bunch of bosh," it's most enjoyable in exclamation form. For example:

> Would you like to see a reboot of a prequel to a remake?
> *Bosh!*
> What did you learn in graduate school?
> *Bosh!*
> What do Democrats and Republicans have in common?
> *Bosh!*

As for its origins, *bosh* is a loan word from Turkish, where it means "worthless." James Justinian Morier's novel *Ayesha, the Maid of Kars,* published in 1834, popularized the word in English.

Bosh also has a rhyming synonym: *tosh.* By any system of measurement, a load of bosh = a bunch of tosh.

Bovril

British "food" product Bovril is a spread made from beef extract; apparently, it's also a hot drink. If that sounds as horrible to you as it does to me, you can understand why *Bovril* is also a generally negative term used specifically to call bullshit.

A 1937 use from the *Bulletin of the Australian English Association* explained that "young men" used the term *Bovril* "whenever they found anything unimpressive." A 1955 mention of "bloody socialistic Bovril" makes the bullshit sense clearer. And a 2003 comment on Amazon UK shows that the term is still around: "It took Targus' nice man on the tech support phone, and a deeper dig in the support site to reveal the companies [sic] initial promise was a load of bovril."

Even a pitcher of balderdash washed down with a bowl of drivel sounds more appetizing than a load—or teaspoon—of Bovril. *Shudder.*

bugaboo

Were you ever afraid of monsters under your bed? Many kids are. At some point you likely realized such monsters were bullshit—but they are also bugaboos.

Originally, a bugaboo was like a boogeyman. This early use from 1740 shows the bugaboo's typical company: "Of Hobgoblins, Rawheads, and Bloody-bones, Buggybows."

Horror innovator Edgar Allan Poe used the term in 1843's "The Premature Burial": "No fustian about church-yards, no bugaboo tales." Since bugaboo tales tend to be bullshit, the word itself became a word for bullshit. The following example from 1959 in *The Listener and BBC Television Review* is a timeless lament about how a simple question can yield meandering mumbo jumbo: "So straightforward an inquiry can produce so rich a harvest of pure bugaboo."

I imagine that's how journalists feel when they interview politicians. Or athletes. Or anyone, really. Bugaboo is abundant.

Bugaboo is also the name of a trendy, overpriced stroller, so parents with strained wallets may have extra reason to appreciate this term.

bull

The chicken or the egg is a tough one, but it should be safe to assume *bullshit* came before *bull*, at least lexically. *Bull* feels like a simple euphemism for *bullshit* that surely came later.

But it didn't.

The word *bullshit* is rather young. It's been turning up only since the early 1900s. But *bullshit*'s roots are much older, and they are in the word *bull*.

The first meaning dates back to the 1600s and is defined by the *Oxford English Dictionary* as a "ludicrous jest." It seems a bull was something like a prank or joke, like if you replaced your buddy's ale with jester sweat while enjoying some wholesome bear-baiting entertainment.

Soon after, the term was used to mean something far closer to bullshit: a "self-contradictory proposition." In this early use, from 1651, you can see the primordial origins of the expression "no bullshit": "It is no Bull, to speake of a Common Peace, in the place of Warre." In other words, proposing peace instead of war ain't horsefeathers.

Around the same time, *bullshit* starts turning up, and *bull* starts to mean nonsense, hot air, lies, and other elements of the bullshit spectrum. This 1932 use from the *Times Literary Supplement* shows some of the range: " 'Bull' is the slang term for a combination of bluff, bravado, 'hot-air', and what we used to call in the Army 'Kidding the troops'."

Speaking of the military, *bull* took on another meaning during the World War II era: anything having to do with superficial appearances, excessive discipline, and mindless routine. Then and now, when you have to do a bunch of meaningless work for appearances' sake, it's bull.

Bull Durham, cush

I'm no movie critic, so I won't suggest *Bull Durham* is bullshit. I can also provide relief to fans: The Kevin Costner film has nothing to do with this term's occasional use as a word for nonsense.

Rather, this is a regional term for nonsense or rubbish

simply because it includes the word *bull*—and because *Bull Durham* is the name of a tobacco brand. Other chew-related words have also made it into the BS lexicon—like *cush,* according to the *Dictionary of American Regional English.*

It makes sense that terms for tobacco you smoke in a pipe or chew in a wad also mean nonsense or rubbish. I don't think anything is more rubbishy than chewed tobacco. Sorry, chew enthusiasts.

bullsh, frogsh

There are a lot of ways to take the obscenity out of *bullshit.* You can call it *bullcrap, bullpoop, bull s—, bull*$#!,* plain ol' *bull,* or *cowyard confetti.* You can also call it *bullsh.*

In J. B. Priestley's 1948 novel *The Linden Tree,* we can see an example of this euphemism: "Look—I'm talking too much—and most of it bullsh, I suppose."

Turns out you can do the same kind of abbreviation for

a not-so-well-known alternative to bullshit: *frogshit,* which sometimes goes by *frogsh* in Australia.

This kind of euphemism by abbreviation can be seen outside of bullshit words, like when you call a motherfucker a *mo-fo* or *muh-fuh.*

bullshit

Since this whole book is about bullshit, this seems like a good place to look at some variations of the word itself.

A bullshitter goes by several names, such as *bullshit artist* or *bullshit merchant.* There are also *bull-shooters, bull-slingers,* and *bull-throwers.* All of the above are likely to take part in a *bullshit session.* Someone who can identify bullshit has a good *bullshit detector.*

In the military, a *bullshit bomber* is a plane that carries out psychological operations, like dropping leaflets or broadcasting propaganda messages. That practice and term emerged in the Vietnam War. Also in the military, a *bullshit band* is a radio frequency used for chitchat.

Euphemisms for *bullshit* include *bullcon, bullcorn, bullcrap, bulldickey, bulldinky, bull dust, bull feathers, bull hockey, bull jive, bull manure, bull muffins, bull pucky, bull roar,* and *bull-sugar.* On *It's Always Sunny in Philadelphia,* sleazebag patriarch Frank Reynolds contributed an uncharacteristically family-friendly term: *bullbird.*

There are also plenty of aphorisms involving bullshit,

such as "Money talks, bullshit walks," "A little bullshit goes a long way," "Bullshit can get you to the top, but it won't keep you there," "Don't bullshit a bullshitter," and "If you can't dazzle them with brilliance, baffle them with bull-shit."

bumf

Bumf would look spot on as a sound effect in a comic book or on the *Batman* TV show. Batman clobbers the Joker: *Bumf!*

But this word is a long way from crime-fighting and clown-punching: It refers to a pile of bullshit paperwork.

Bumf is an abbreviation of *bumfodder* that retains that word's most literal sense: toilet paper. That's the first meaning of *bumf,* which has been seen in print since the late 1800s.

From toilet paper *bumf* spread to other printed matter that deserves to be crumpled and flushed. *Bumf* can refer to reams of paperwork, especially paperwork that's a rigmarole or ballyhoo. The term doesn't convey much respect in uses like this 1938 example from Evelyn Waugh's 1938 novel *Scoop:* "I shall get a daily pile of bumf from the Ministry of Mines." If comedy classic *Office Space* had been a British production, it likely would have included this word. TPS reports are classic bumf.

Bumf is also used more broadly, expanding beyond a pile of craptastic paper to any pile of crap. Recent British publications have included mentions of "promotional bumf," "press bumf," "PR bumf," "official bumf," and "marketing bumf." So *bumf* works well when describing the omnipresent, desperate, cloying world of advertising and branding—which, in a more honest world, would be called bumfing.

bunch, load

BS has a way of contaminating everything it touches, including two innocent words used to quantify it.

Word expert Jonathon Green identifies *bunch* as U.S. campus slang and an abbreviation for "bunch of bullshit." Green finds a 1901 use that suggests the term may have been around in the previous century too: " 'Oh, bunch!' exclaimed the second tennis boy in the slang of the period, which was the early eighties."

This is quite similar to the term *load,* another abbreviated expression. "That's a real load" is a pithier and cleaner way to say something like "That's the biggest load of horseshit in the history of horses and shit."

bunk

Where did *bunk* come from? Unlike so many other words, it wasn't coined on *Seinfeld,* though it was memorably discussed on that show:

> ELAINE: If anyone needs any medical advice, Elaine met a doctor. And he's unattached.
> JERRY: I thought the whole dream of dating a doctor was debunked.
> ELAINE: No, it's not debunked, it's totally bunk.
> JERRY: Isn't bunk bad? Like, that's a lot of bunk.
> GEORGE: No, something is bunk and then you debunk it.
> JERRY: What?
> ELAINE: Huh?
> GEORGE: I think.
> ELAINE: Look, I'm dating a doctor and I like it. Let's just move on.

For the real origin, we have to look back to February 25, 1820, the birthday of *bunk.*

On that day Congress was supposed to discuss the Missouri Question. Felix Walker of Buncombe County, North

Carolina, like so many other politicians before and since, preferred to discuss matters related to his own constituents. Despite the disapproval of his colleagues, Walker insisted on making a speech for Buncombe.

His words, or at least his vehemence, were memorable, because "to speak for Buncombe" soon became an idiom for political BS of the pandering sort.

As tends to happen, the term shifted further. *Buncombe* became *bunkum,* then simply *bunk.*

bushlips

Remember when the first President Bush said, "Read my lips: no new taxes," and then there were new taxes anyway? That's the origin of this word, which sounds a little like a lisped version of *bullshit.*

Texas senator Lloyd Bentsen—who was also famous for telling Dan Quayle, "Senator, I served with Jack Kennedy. I knew Jack Kennedy. Jack Kennedy was a friend of mine. Senator, you're no Jack Kennedy"—spread the term. Bentsen, quoting an unknown person, said: "As one of our colleagues recently put it, this Republican pledge of no new taxes is pure bushlips. It's bushlips when the president says, 'No new taxes,' and sends a budget requiring the Finance Committee to raise $20 billion in new revenues: $15 billion in taxes and $5 billion in user fees."

Like so many other words tied to specific political events, *bushlips* did not succeed beyond a brief moment. But it still has a place in lexical history: It was the American Dialect Society's first Word of the Year in 1990.

bushwa

This North American term is a straightforward euphemism for bullshit. Well, sort of.

Bushwa, which started popping up in the early 1900s, might be an insulting variation of *bourgeois*, which *bushwa*'s sound greatly resembles. That origin isn't airtight, but *bushwa* fits right into the bullshit lexicon, where it makes a perfect abbreviation/euphemism. *Bushwa* shortens *bull* to *bu* and *shit* to *sh*, but *bush*—notwithstanding the word *bushlips*—would be an odd term for BS. It needs the final syllable, *wa*, to become a satisfying two-syllable exclamation.

In fact, this term seems to be used most often as an exclamation, though not always. This 1959 use from Ross Macdonald's novel *The Galton Case* is pretty straightforward: "If you're a detective, what was all that bushwa about Hollywood and Sunset Boulevard?" I wager a big part of being a detective is separating the evidence from the bushwa.

casuistry

Often, *casuistry* is simply a synonym for *sophistry*. But it is also another specific type of grade-A baloney.

In fact, this specific sense is related to specifics—or rather, cases. Originally, *casuistry* was used by religious folks who tried to relate spiritual and moral edicts to real-life examples, especially ones that created a conflict. That's a fairly practical pursuit, but the term took on a negative spin. *Casuistry* ended up meaning a kind of two-faced bullpucky marked by evasiveness and dishonesty.

Think about a spouse trying to justify infidelity or a plagiarist explaining how someone else's words ended up in his article: If you're trying to explain why something wrong is okay because of special circumstances, you're coughing up a big ball of casuistry.

An 1836 use from *The Penny Cyclopedia* states that casuistry "has been termed not inaptly the 'art of quibbling with God.'" You don't have to be religious to think quibbling with God is not a great idea. This idea of quibbling, nit-picking, or rationalizing became part of the word's DNA.

This word continues to be used in religious circles, even the highest of such circles. In a 2014 interview Pope Francis said, "Avoid just scratching the surface of a subject. The temptation to solve problems by casuistry is a mistake, a simplification of deep things. This is what the Pharisees did with their very superficial theology."

"A simplification of deep things" is a strong description of casuistry by a pope known for cutting through the bullshit.

clacket

A clacket sounds like a racket, and it is: It's a racket made up of chitchatting, jibber-jabbering, whitter-whattering voices.

Since the 1500s this has been a noun and a verb for excessive talking. You get a sense of the term from the following 1579 *Oxford English Dictionary* example: "Three houres space wil not bee ynough for them to clackket out halfe that they would say." Translation: "These geezers are so unconcise and twaddlesome they could talk for three hours, three days, eternity, you name it."

clamjamphrie

This poetic-sounding word doesn't have a very poetic meaning: It refers to stuff that's insignificant or meaningless.

The *Oxford English Dictionary* suggests the origin may have something to do with a Scottish clan and the word *jampher:* a Scottish term for someone with a big mouth, a small work ethic, or both. But like so much etymology, that's not certain. Word origins can be trickier to trace than a drug dealer's conversation on a disposable cell phone.

What is known is that this word is a close synonym of *trumpery.* So it's best applied to bullshit of the trivial, trifling sort.

This is an obscure word, but it still pops up from time to time. A 2011 article in the *National Interest* includes it: "But the clamjamphrie of conservatives who insist on smearing Muslim-Americans as amounting to a fifth column have found their issue, and won't let it go." And a 2015 article in the *Scotsman* uses the word with appropriate alliteration: "This is where the debate about Saturday's cacophonous clamjamphrie has gone."

claptrap, clapter

Claptrap pretty much defines itself: It's a trap for claps. Claptrap is the kind of blather that politicians, performers, and other public speakers spew to make their audiences slap their hands together like trained seals.

Claptrap has been around since the early 1700s, and over time it evolved from meaning public and theatrical nonsense to meaning any type of nonsense. Amusing variations include *claptrappery, claptrappily, claptrappish,* and *claptrappy.*

A recent word is a close relative of claptrap: *clapter.*

In Mike Sacks' *Poking a Dead Frog: Conversations with Today's Top Comedy Writers,* longtime *Saturday Night Live* head writer James Downey describes a comedy pet peeve: "What has bothered me most for the last few years is that kind of lazy, political comedy, very safe but always pretending to be brave, that usually gets what my colleague Seth Meyers calls 'clapter.' Clapter is that earnest applause, with a few 'whoops' thrown in, that lets you know the audience agrees with you, but what you just said wasn't funny enough to actually make them laugh."

The lesson: If you're trying to get claps, you probably don't deserve them.

cobblers

This British term looks odd at first. Though the word is old-fashioned, there doesn't seem to be any direct connection between the hardworking cobbler and major-league bull-shit.

And there isn't. Thanks to Cockney rhyming slang, *cobbler's awls* (leather-piercing tools) becomes a term for *balls,* both sporting and masculine. As demonstrated by the lexical journeys of *balls, bollocks,* and *nuts,* any word for a testicle is likely to become a word for nonsense.

Oxford English Dictionary examples include phrases such as "all cobblers" and "load of cobblers." A 1970 use from Alfred Draper's novel *Swansong for a Rare Bird* displays an attitude common among nonfashionistas and nudists: "Why all this cobblers about clothes?"

codswallop

The origin of this term for BS is very unclear, though there are theories. Some say it's named for Hiram Codd, a British maker of soft drinks. The idea is that *codswallop* was used insultingly by beer drinkers to refer to soft drinks—not only because they lacked the wallop of beer but also because *wallop* was a word for beer. However, this etymology appears to be codswallop itself. Or, as British word guy Michael Quinion puts it, "This story reeks of the approach to word history called folk etymology": a too-neat explanation made up after the fact. Early spellings don't support this or any other appealing story, and we just don't know the origin story of *codswallop*. Maybe it came from the same guys who did Stonehenge.

Regardless of origin, this term has been used as a word for nonsense or BS since the 1950s. A 1959 use from Ray Galton and Alan Simpson's *The Best of Hancock* demands, "Don't give me that old codswallop." A 1963 use from the *Radio Times* shows *codswallop* was firmly within the lexicon of bullshit: "Just branding a programme as 'rubbish', 'tripe', or—there are a lot of these—'codswallop', gives little indication of what moved the viewer to write."

Like other three-syllable words for bullshit—*balderdash, poppycock, tommyrot*—this term is a delicious mouthful with an old-timey feel.

confetti

Just as *hockey* and *pucky* turn up in several BS euphemisms in the United States, *confetti* has the same multipurpose function in Australia, where it's part of several ridiculous terms: *cow confetti, cowyard confetti, farmyard confetti,* and *Flemington confetti.*

The origin of these terms isn't entirely clear, but at least one of them is directly related to paper. *Flemington confetti* comes from the Flemington racecourse, where after a race the course is littered with losing betting slips (as well as the hopes and dreams of gamblers). Since those slips are worthless, *Flemington confetti* came to be a word for any worthless thing: nonsense, rubbish, bullshit. Here's a 1951 use from Aussie Dal Stivens' political novel *Jimmy Brockett:* "You could pull the wad over his eyes if you talked enough Flemington confetti about the woes of the working class."

These terms are among the most colorful and evasive in the bullshit lexicon, as seen in a 1973 article from the *Sydney Sun-Herald:* "Lots of farmyard confetti has been spoken and written about this young man's selection." *Green's Dictionary of Slang* records a similar term in 1981 from another Australian source, in which *cowyard confetti* is referred to as an old-fashioned term used "in polite company."

From these Australian uses you could make up plenty of variations: *bull confetti, horse confetti, dog confetti, Congress confetti.* Those terms would be useful when someone's throwing a bullshit parade.

crap, crapola

Like the many forms of *shit,* the word *crap* and its various forms are often used to suggest bullshit. In particular, *crapping* can be a type of lying or flattery. If you're crapping me, you're manipulating me. A crap artist is a bullshit artist.

The most popular crap-related BS word is probably *crapola,* which borrows a suffix from words like *payola* and *shinola.* A use in Larry Heinemann's 1986 novel *Paco's Story* gives a good sense of the word's meaning and flavor: "I don't want no chickenshit Marine Corps crapola."

Rarer variations include *craperoo* and *crappadooley.* You might enjoy these words if, as the Dude said in *The Big Lebowski,* you're not into the whole brevity thing, man.

Even if you know shit from shinola, it's hard to tell crap from craperoo.

crapspackle

The writers of *Futurama* loved to invent new words. These words fit into many categories, including new inventions (*career chip, probulator, truthoscope, foodamatron, gizmometer, diamondillium*), exclamations (*spluh, guh, zookabarooka, abracaduh*), general insults (*spleezball, scazzwag, scum-pile, duncebag, creepwad*), robo-insults (*scuzzbot, boltbag, soup-can*), and insults for humans (*fleshwad, organ sack, skintube, meatloaf, pork pouch, beefball, skinbag, coffin-stuffer*).

They also coined words for bullshit.

These words were typically used by the character Professor Farnsworth, the senile founder of the Planet Express delivery company. Mostly these terms played on established BS words. Even in the future world of the show, there's no mistaking the meaning behind these exclamations: Blithery-poop! Baldercrap! Twaddle-cock! Drivel-poop!

And: Crapspackle!

The intention behind this word was probably pure absurdity, but it makes a lot of sense. Spackle smooths over a damaged surface, such as cracks in plaster. So if you're spouting crapspackle, you've filled in the gaps of your story or argument with pure crap.

crock

Let's pause for a moment to celebrate the word *crock*. It's a fantastically satisfying word to say, perhaps because it has sounds in common with *cock, crap,* and *fuck.* "What a crock!" is an underused way to call bullshit, and we should all be using it more often on Facebook and in job interviews.

This term has one of the simplest origins. A crock has been a pot since at least A.D. 1000. In the mid-1940s *crock of shit* and just plain *crock* began emerging as terms for BS or nonsense. For example, this 1945 use from *Yank* magazine: " 'That,' observed Winters softly, 'is a crock.' " As with *load*—as in "What a load!"—the bullshit is implied.

donkey dust

This is a Massachusetts term recorded in the *Dictionary of American Regional English.* Like *cowyard confetti, mule fritters,* and *horse apples,* this is a pretty straightforward term for bullshit—well, straightforward for a euphemism.

Green's Dictionary of Slang traces the term back to at least 1956. Of course, *dust* is a word with a long history and plenty of grimy, dirty meanings, so it's never been that far from bullshit.

A 2010 post by religious blogger Barbara Laymon uses and explains the term: "Yesterday someone told me that I was full of donkey dust . . . donkey dust as in 'Barbara you are full of crap.'" In Roberta Rosenfield Wells' 2001 novel *Moonshadow,* a character hollers, "Donkey dust!"

when a groping jerk suggests his handsiness was spurred by flirting.

Like *all gas and gaiters* and *bunch of bullshit,* this term has alliteration going for it. That alone should make it a candidate for wider use.

doodad, doodaddle

Doodad and *doodaddle* are part of one of the most folksy and fun vocabularies: indefinite words. These terms—like *thingamajig, hooziewhatsit,* and *dooflicker*—refer to any gadget you can't quite name.

Doodad and *doodaddle* have also been used for any small object, which was the beginning of their canoe ride down Bullshit River. Tiny, decorative objects—due to their lack of significance—often share terms with bullshit.

A use from Harold L. Davis' 1935 novel *Honey in the Horn* shows this word can be used not only for perplexing objects but also for confounding verbiage: "Why don't you explain to these people how it happened, in place of all this doodaddle about witnesses?" Another familiar construction can be seen in Raymond Chandler's 1958 novel *Playback:* "Cut the doodads." Or, as a wise man once said, cut the shit.

Indefinite words and BS words have a lot of common ground. The infix *ma*—which is part of words like *thingamajig* and *whatchamajigger*—suggests something pretty close to "What is this bullshit?"

doo-doo

Most words for *shit,* including *shit* itself, can be used as synonyms for *bullshit.* This includes even the most childish of words: *doo-doo.*

This word feels simple and primal enough to be centuries old, but it's been spotted in print only since 1954, when it is first shown displaying literal and metaphorical meanings. By 1973 there are examples moving closer to bullshit, like this sentence from the *Burlington (North Carolina) Daily Times News:* "You call that living? I call it doo-doo."

Fiction master Kurt Vonnegut combined BS terms in 1990's *Hocus Pocus,* which included the phrase "crocks of doo-doo." The bullshit-laden topic of ghosts also attracts doo-doo, as seen in this use from Emily Christoff Flowers' 2012 book *The Ghost Journal: Memoirs of a Ghost Tour Guide in Williamsburg, Virginia:* "Of course I always thought it [ghost sightings] was a bunch of doo doo, but found it highly entertaining." Jerry Seinfeld has said there's no such thing as fun for the whole family, but the word *doo-doo* comes close.

Unfortunately, silly little words like *doo-doo* don't get much respect, and that's a shame. As Isaac Goldberg put it in 1938's *The Wonder of Words:* "In the dawn of language, the bow-wows and the pooh-poohs and even the ding-dongs must have served man well."

double Dutch

You may know double Dutch as jump-rope game, but it's also pure gibberish.

Dutch itself has been used, since at least the mid-1800s, as a term for nonsense, probably influenced by a dismissive attitude toward the Dutch language. Alliteration plus exaggeration led to the term *double Dutch*. This 1879 use by Charles Haddon Spurgeon shows the term was still directly tied to a mistrust of other languages: "The preacher preaches double Dutch or Greek, or something of the sort." You could think of this term as a more colorful and prejudiced version of *doubletalk* or *doublespeak*.

Double Dutch is related to other Dutch-bashing terms such as *in Dutch* (in trouble) and *do a Dutch* (flee or commit suicide).

doublespeak, doubletalk

Here's a useful couple of words for bullshit that is, in some sense, two-pronged.

Either can involve plain talk mixed with gibberish, words that can be taken two ways, or straight-up lying.

A good example of doublespeak or doubletalk is sometimes called dog-whistle politics. This is when a politician uses coded language to send a message to certain constituents. For example, most politicians are decent enough (or at least smart enough) to avoid blatant racism, but they might offer subtle appeals to racist voters—such as speaking against anything "urban," which is often a euphemism for African American. That's the dog whistle, and the hope is that only the intended audience—racists—will hear it.

Doublespeak, which has been around since the 1950s, sounds like a George Orwell term, but it's not: It's just very similar to Orwellisms such as *doublethink* and *newspeak.*

dreck

Yiddish *drek* and German *dreck,* which spawned English *dreck,* are pretty straightforward words for rubbish, which clings to every spoke of the bullshit wheel.

This one-syllable word's hard ending sound makes it a powerful, appealing word to say. It's still commonly used, and it seems to have particular appeal for people writing about popular culture, which is about 91.4 percent dreck, studies show. For example, in the *Huffington Post,* William Bradley recently had this to say about *Star Trek*'s fiftieth anniversary: "There's a fair amount of dreck in there, especially in *Voyager* which I often struggled to get through." A review of *The Wedding Ringer* by Matt Brunson in *Connect Savannah* includes a similar use: "The only ingredient that makes this swampy stew even palatable is Hart, who continues to deliver inspired comic performances in dreck such as *Grudge Match, Ride Along* and now this." *Dreck* is a perfect word for such "swampy stews," no matter the art form.

Given Hollywood's obsession with sequels, reboots, prequels, and reimaginings, there's more dreck than ever. By the time this book is your hands, it might even be time for *Star Wars: The Dreck Awakens* or *Batman v Superman: Dawn of Dreck.*

drivel

If you hear about someone spouting drivel, it sounds a lot like verbal diarrhea, doesn't it? Well, that's exactly what the term originally meant. From the fourteenth century to the eighteenth, *drivel* referred to any spittle or other bodily business frothing from someone's mouth.

Perhaps in response to the timeless advice "Say it, don't spray it," *drivel* took a turn in the eighteenth century and began to mean what it does today: nonliquid garbage spewing from someone's mouth.

Though old, *drivel* has never faded in popularity. In early 2015 recent publications include mentions of "meaningless drivel," "political drivel," "toxic drivel," "racist drivel," "utter drivel," "illiterate drivel," "celebrity culture drivel," and—perhaps the most common—"inane online drivel." In a time when every person's thoughts can be broadcast to the world, there's probably more drivel available than ever before.

A rare, old word that harks back to the literal form of *drivel* is *drivel-bib,* which is just what it sounds like. This word is ready for a comeback. Next time someone won't shut up, tell them they forgot their drivel-bib.

drool

If *drivel* isn't salivary enough for you, how about *drool*?

Like other watery words—such as *slop* and *slush*—*drool* is often a sentimental type of BS.

Though *drool* is usually its own plural form, there are exceptions. In H. S. Harrison's 1911 novel *Queed,* a character remarks, "Say, Doc, I been readin' them reformatory drools of yours." In other words, "With respect, Doctor, I've been reading the awful crap you've been writing."

Drools as a plural noun sounds odd to my ears, but it is useful. Zeus knows the world is full of drools.

eyewash

Eyewash has had a rather literal meaning since the 1700s: stuff used to wash your eyes. Eventually it came to mean stuff that pulls the wool over your eyes too.

In the 1800s *eyewash* became military slang for the kind of outward show that will pass inspection but might be bogus or deceiving: like a made bed that conceals contraband. A 1976 use from the *Army Quarterly* mentions "contempt for eyewash, spit and polish and ceremonial." Like spit and polish, eyewash is pleasing only at a glance. It's pretty much lipstick on a pig.

From there the term mimicked *hogwash* and became a broader, if not common, term for BS. A 2012 use from an Australian newspaper mentions a claim dismissed as a "bagful of eyewash." That's a colorful way to say "bunch of crap."

You can also be an eyewasher, which is the kind of showy person who can't stop blah-blahing and posing. This 1997 use by Vitalii Iosifovich Gol'danskii shows this meaning in action: "I would call them eyewashers. They try to present their proposals such that, even though completely unrelated, they appear to have something to do with SDI." Apparently, eyewashers knew as much about the Strategic Defense Initiative as I do.

You say eyewasher, I say bullshitter.

fee-faw-fum

Fee-faw-fum—and variations such as *fe fi fo fum*—started out as the language of a giant, specifically the one in the tale originally called "Jack the Giant Killer." As with many fables and fairy tales, the origin is tough to place, but the story is quoted in *King Lear:* "His word was stil fy fo and fum, I smell the bloud of a British man."

Shakespeare aside, such tales were meant for kids, and this nonsensical phrase took on a childish meaning. The *Oxford English Dictionary* defines it as "nonsense, fitted only to terrify children."

The first such use is by John Dryden in his 1690 comedy *Amphitryon:* "The bloody Villain is at his fee, fa, fum, already." *Fee-faw-fum* and its variations became shorthand for cartoonish villains and their dastardly nonsense, much like mustache twirling and kitten stroking today. *Fee-faw-fum* can also mean other forms of bullshit, as seen in journalist Albany William Fonblanque's 1830 book *England Under Seven Administrations,* which dismissively refers to "the fee-fa-fum style of rhetoric."

felgercarb

Science fiction often features euphemisms, partly to show that its characters live in a different world and partly to get around censors.

Battlestar Galactica (*BSG*) launched a very successful euphemism for the F-word: *frak.* That word was coined on the original 1970s series and used heavily on the reimagined show in the 2000s.

A far less successful *BSG* euphemism was *felgercarb,* which meant bullshit. Back in the 1978 pilot episode, "Saga of a Star World," our roguish hero Starbuck tells Cassiopeia, "You certainly have a way of cutting through the felgercarb."

Felgercarb was not used in dialogue on the new *BSG*, probably because it has no ring to it whatsoever, unlike *frak*. But it did appear just once—as the name of a toothpaste brand.

Other than that, *felgercarb* lives on in the vocabulary of hard-core geeks. A 2012 tweet by @DyNama keeps the *felgercarb* flame alive: "Millions of boomers are entering retirement w/permanent injuries because they believed the felgercarb about exercise for exercise sake."

Presumably, this tweet refers to baby boomers, not Cylon copies of the *BSG* character Boomer. Evil robots don't need cardio.

fiddle-faddle, fiddledeedee, fiddlesticks

The poor fiddle. Thanks to the weird and wooly evolution of English, it is without question the official musical instrument of bullshit.

Fiddle-faddle is the same type of word as *mumbo jumbo*, but it has a decidedly different meaning. Mumbo jumbo is big words and overstuffed lingo. Fiddle-faddle is the type of bullshit that's trivial, trifling, and insignificant. In 1848 Francis Darwin, in a letter to his famous father, Charles, wrote, "Describing species of birds and shells, &c., is all fiddle-faddle." Fathers of the world, take note: Even the inventor of Darwinism got accused of twaddle by his son.

You can also say "Fiddledeedee!" or "Fiddlesticks!" when you hear a bunch of bull.

It's not clear why *fiddle* is such a bullshit-friendly word. *Fiddle* has occasionally referred to a swindle, which might have something to do with it. Maybe it's just the sound of *fiddle,* which is so similar to *diddle.* Anything in the ballpark of diddly-squat and diddly-poo is not likely to inspire much respect.

flannel

I don't think food is more nonsensical than clothing, but it does seem like more BS words come from the menu than from the wardrobe. Here's an exception.

Since the 1500s flannel has been a fabric, and the word was also used to describe a specific piece of fabric, generally not an exalted piece of cloth. Often a flannel was simply a washcloth. That lowly meaning may have something to do with the detour of this word down Bullshit Boulevard.

You can also be a flannel-mouth. A 1934 definition from *Webster's* shows the term has a few related senses: "*Flannel-mouthed,* orig., talking thickly with or as with a brogue; now, smooth-spoken; oily-tongued;—often contemptuous." As that definition suggests, this term was also associated with the Irish, not always in a complimentary manner.

A 1970 use from the *Daily Telegraph* displays a common advertising pitch: "This coupon will bring you our 'all facts—no flannel' brochure telling you all about us." "All facts, no flannel" is a classic anti-BS slogan along the lines of "Less talk, more rock."

flapdoodle

Though it sounds like a Ned Flanders–ism, this rare word for crapola has several variations that go back to the late 1800s rather than to *The Simpsons*.

Mark Twain used *flapdoodle* in *Adventures of Huckleberry Finn:* "Well, by and by the king he gets up and comes forward a little, and works himself up and slobbers out a speech, all full of tears and flapdoodle." When tears are accompanied by flapdoodle, don't trust the tears.

Flapdoodle can also be a verb. "To flapdoodle" is to bull-shit in a particularly meandering way. If you're flapdoodling, you're not getting to the point, or you're taking so many divergences that it's getting ridiculous.

Like so many other BS words, it can also be part of an exclamation, such as "Fudge and flapdoodle!"

flubdub

What's the hubbub? Often, it's a flubdub. This super-fun word is rare, but it's concise and punchy.

The *Dictionary of American Regional English* records "legalistic flubdub" and "amateur flubdub." Those uses express two common sentiments, since people generally dislike lawyers and dilettantes who don't know what they're doing.

The *Oxford English Dictionary* defines *flubdub* as "bombastic or inept language," and examples cover a wide range of BS, from politics to fortune-telling. The examples also indicate that *flubdub* often has a friend, as the word turns up in groupings such as "flub-dub and guff," "fuss and flubdub," and "flubdub and nonsense and gush." It seems people use *flubdub* when there's so much bullshit that one word can't describe it all.

In Massachusetts a *flubdub* can also be an apple dumpling— one you eat, not a horse apple.

fluff

Fluff has had several meanings related to things soft, feathery, or furry, like the stuffing in a pillow or the coat of a Papillon. When it comes to BS, *fluff* refers to empty, unnecessary words that have little substance but often too much sentimentality. Hallmark cards—which are synonymous with oversticky sentiment—are all fluff.

A 1986 issue of the *New Yorker* refers to a "fluff specialist" as the kind of reporter who tackles hard-hitting stories such as "the new baby giraffe" at the zoo.

A fluff specialist is the bullshit artist of the journalism world.

flummery

Flummery is bullshit with an upside, at least for fragile egos: It's the flattering sort of hooey.

That meaning comes from *flummery*'s original sense as a dessert, specifically a super-sweet dish that contained eggs, flour, and milk. Since flummery was so sweet, its name made an easy transition to words that are a little too sweet to be trusted.

Just as a bag of candy soothes a sweet tooth while providing no nutrition, a tale of flummery may soothe a tender ego without facts. The food and words are both empty. Some advice in early 2015 about how to succeed on Twitter by social media expert Adrian Dayton is wise: "Don't share self-promotional flummery or tout your successes; share information that will help people do their jobs better; that gives practical advice on tricky legal concepts." Flummery's not useful or nutritious: It's the corn syrup of words.

Flummery, like most successful words, has procreated. There's a rare verb form: *flummer*. If you flummer someone, you're sweet-talking them. Colorful, folksy synonyms for *flummery* include *flummerdiddle* and *flummadiddle*.

Diddle links these words to other rare BS words like *tara-*

diddle and *diddle-daddle,* which are also a bunch of fiddle-faddle.

folderol

This word made a straightforward movement from music to mumbo jumbo: It originally referred to a nonsensical song refrain. "Lalalalalalala" and "na na na na" are literal folderol. Such sounds don't make a lot of sense, and the word (first appearing in the early 1700s) spread from one kind of nonsense to others.

This is a rather old-fashioned word, but it turns up now and then, including in the 2005 song "A Better Version of Me" by Fiona Apple. Awards shows are like Beethoven symphonies of bullshit, and after the 2015 Oscars, Hank Stuever pulled out this appropriate word: "Go-to awards show host Neil Patrick Harris couldn't deliver quite all the thrills needed to get through the three-hour, 38-minute Oscar folderol without a yawn." Man, who could?

four-flusher

This word for a bullshitter comes from the world of human waste: It's named for a bowel movement so monumental that only four flushes can send it down the sewer. So before you call someone a four-flusher, make sure they've dumped a severe and catastrophic load of bullshit on you.

Nah. That's crap.

This word has no relationship to the bathroom or the human body, except perhaps the hand, since it comes from the realm of poker. This term's roots go back to the late 1800s, when *four flush* is first recorded: a hand that's one short of a flush and therefore pretty much worthless. If you call or raise with a four flush, you're bluffing. You're also a four-flusher.

This led to *four-flushing*'s being used as a verb in the late 1800s and early 1920s for various types of bluffing. That sense was used in George Ade's 1896 novel *Artie:* " 'I thought he was going to fight.' 'Not that boy. He was four-flushin'.'" I reckon four-flushin' is in the same ballpark as trash-talkin'.

At the same time, a person known for talking this kind of trash came to be known as a four-flusher, which the *Oxford English Dictionary* defines as "a pretender, braggart, humbug." A four-flusher, just like a bluffer in poker, can't back up his boasts. That sentence should probably be gender neutral, but you have to admit four-flushing sounds like typical dude behavior.

fribble

No, not a tribble, *Star Trek* fans. But a fribble isn't any more serious than the furry little pests called tribbles. Throughout its history this word referred to the frivolous and insignificant.

First it applied to a person who is a silly goof-off. From people the term spread to similarly trifling things and ideas. In his 1840 novel *Catherine*, William Thackeray uses the expression "lies and fribble nonsense." "Fribble nonsense" is fairly redundant, much as "mumbo-jumbo jibber-jabber" or "bunk malarkey" would be.

In George Augustus Sala's 1859 novel *Twice Round the Clock,* he used the term with another silly-sounding word: "the innumerable whim-whams and fribble-frabble of fashion."

Today we'd probably say "the endless bullshit of fashion."

fudge

Some BS words are rather unappetizing, like *balderdash, balductum,* and *horseshit.* Others aren't quite so disgusting but may not be huge crowd-pleasers, like *pickles* and *rhubarb.*

But who doesn't like fudge?

It turns out the origins of *fudge* as a word for nonsense have nothing to do with the sweet treat. *Fudge* started popping up in the late 1700s in the sense of fudging the numbers or facts. The chocolate delight known as fudge didn't exist. Apparently *fudge* was an alteration of *fadge:* a now-archaic word for making things fit.

An 1876 use in Frances Eleanor Trollope's *A Charming Fellow* could easily be updated: "Anything of consequence to say? Fudge! He is coming begging." Today you could say: "This jerk with a clipboard just wants to spread awareness? Bullshit! He wants a credit card number."

It's not clear why *fudge* made the leap from bullshit to confections in the late 1800s. I think it's safe to say that if the chocolate kind of fudge had come first, the rubbish kind of fudge might not exist at all. Good fudge tastes like anything but baloney.

full of it

Are you full? That's a good thing if you've just eaten. But much of the time *full* has to do with being engorged by one of the many varieties of bullshit.

Full of shit and *full of crap* are two very common expressions, but this construction is so well understood, you can replace those fecal words with the ultrageneral pronoun *it*. When someone is full of it, everyone knows what *it* is.

This expression goes back to at least the 1930s, and it's very common today. In some headlines from early 2015, you can see its usefulness:

"Study: Most People Think Scientists Are Full
  of It"
"Dr. Dre—Suge's Full of It . . . I Never Asked for a
  Peace Summit"
"Science Says Your FitBit's Full of It"

Scientists, rappers, and exercise gadgets don't have a
lot in common, but it seems each is a productive source of
bullshit.

funny business, monkey business

Funny business is usually tricky, not humorous. That's certainly the meaning used in *The Big Lebowski* when a group of
nihilists—who have faked a kidnapping—implore hapless
stoner Jeffrey Lebowski to deliver the ransom money with
"no funny business." (Please read those words in the ridiculous German accent used in the film. In fact, please read
this whole book that way.)

People have been talking about funny business—which
first meant the jester-type antics of a professional funny
person—since the late 1800s. *Monkey business* has been
around a little longer, and the 1952 movie *Monkey Business*
is a good reminder of the term's essence. IMDb summarizes
the plot: "A chemist finds his personal and professional life
turned upside down when one of his chimpanzees finds the
fountain of youth."

It's best to reserve this term for similar levels of craziness, like if your poodle discovered the Ark of the Covenant or your cat signed a treaty with alien lizard people from space.

galimatias

English has a lot of folksy words for a hodgepodge or mishmash—like, well, *hodgepodge* and *mishmash*. Add *galimatias* to the list. This French word migrated to English in the mid-1600s, and it refers to garbled gibberish.

This 1824 use from Henry Crabb Robinson's *Diary, Reminiscences, and Correspondence* partly explains it: "Now it seemed to me that Mr. C—— had no opinions, only words, for his assertions seemed a mere *galimatias*." That's typical of many sorts of bullshit: words are abundant, but sense or truth is lacking. There's a lot of fluff and flubdub obscuring the point (or lack of a point).

This word is related to *gallimaufry,* another French word for jumbled, mixed-up clusterfraks.

gammon

Gammon is possibly related to *backgammon,* particularly the sense of *gammon* as a type of victory worth double points. A gammon, whether a scam or BS, is an example of running a game on someone.

This disreputable word originally meant an accomplice who creates a distraction facilitating a theft. If you spill a drink while I steal a wallet, you're my gammon. This use has been around since the early 1700s.

Later that century *gammon* evolved into a word for more subtle dishonesty, as in this 1781 use in a book on manners by actor and lecturer George Parker: "I thought myself pretty much a master of *Gammon,* but the Billingsgate eloquence of Mrs. P—— not only exceeded me, but outdid all that I had ever known eloquent in that way." Such verbal gammon is close to sophistry or other verbal bamboozlement.

From there *gammon* gravitated toward various sorts of nonsense and bullshit. Charles Dickens uses the term in this sense in 1837's *The Pickwick Papers:* "Some people maintains that an Englishman's house is his castle. That's gammon."

Gammon can also combine with *spinach* in an idiom similar to "stuff and nonsense." This expression isn't exactly common, but it pops up once in a while, as in this *Daily Telegraph* article from 2012: "Lots of stuff about level playing fields and EU employment legislation. To which I say gammon and spinach!"

Though spinach is rather healthy, gammon and spinach exceed the recommended daily requirements for bullshit.

gentleman cow

A gentleman cow is, simply, a bull. So why not say so? Because the word *bull* was tarnished due to the association with bullshit. Better to be safe and avoid the B-word altogether. On linguistics blog *Language Log,* Roger Shuy discusses his experience gathering data for the *Linguistic Atlas of the United States and Canada.* Of his fieldwork in rural Illinois, Shuy writes:

When I asked the old farmers what they called the male species of bovine animal, I made good use of my city-bred ignorance by phasing my question, "What do you call a male cow?" That always brought a smile, along with a bit of sympathy for my ignorance. But it yielded a good answer anyway, which was as likely to be "gentleman cow" as "bull." The Victorian era lingered in the minds of the "gentleman cow" speakers, along with "white meat" for the breast of chickens, "cut" or "alter" for castrate, and other delicate verbal detours around anything that even hinted of things sexual.

This sense led to *gentleman cow*'s being used occasionally—often humorously—as a term for bullshit too. If you're reluctant to tell a friend or coworker they're bullshitting you, this term is worth a try. A sentence like "I'm sorry, but you just served me a platter of gentleman cow with a side of meadow muffins" will make your point and defuse the situation too.

Gentleman cow is reminiscent of other euphemistic terms such as *gentleman in brown* (a bedbug) and *gentlemen who pays the rent* (a pig).

gibberish

This is unquestionably one of the top synonyms for bullshit, but it is a specific type. Gibberish is complete and utter nonsense. In fact, most of the time it is even more nonsensical than nonsense.

"The moon is made of green cheese" is nonsense. "Yabba dabba bourbon giddyup synergy" is gibberish.

Here's a quite poetic denunciation of gibberish in 1653 from François Rabelais, who was a well-known Renaissance writer and doctor: "the malarkey tattle, and fond fibs, seditiously raised between the gibblegablers, and Accursian gibberish-mongers." The words *tattle* and *fibs* indicate that *gibberish* can be similar to gossip, another common type of bullshit.

Gibberish is also closely related to *jibber-jabber* and a rarer reduplicative word: *hibber-jibber.*

gibble-gabble

"What's that gibble-gabble?"

This word, which resembles the gobbling of a turkey, is reserved for chattering that doesn't say much of anything. And, in fact, the history of *gibble-gabble* is often intertwined with animals.

Specifically, *gibble-gabble,* like its root *gabble,* has referred to the sounds of geese. That naturally led *gabble* and *gibble-gabble* to be used for human sounds that were as senseless, annoying, and meaningless as a goose's honking.

This word dates from at least 1600. In the 1769 poem "Trinculo's Trip to the Jubilee," the word is used and explained: "Soon was heard a gibble-gabble, Neither harmony or sense."

You can hear an echo of several other bullshit words here, including *gibberish* and *babble*. It's also a perfect rhyme for *bibble-babble*.

Is bibble-babble gibble-gabbier than jibber-jabber? Any definitive answer would be bunkum-junkum.

gobbledygook

Have you ever been called a turkey? This fairly innocent and childish insult is part of the background of this word. Just as the gobble-gobble of a turkey is generally not considered intelligent discourse, gobbledygook is pure nonsense.

On his *World Wide Words* site, Michael Quinion sleuthed this word's origin. It seems Texas lawyer, Democratic congressman, and alliterative name-haver Maury Maverick coined the word, which first appeared in the *New York Times Magazine* on May 21, 1944. Maverick was complaining about his colleagues' obscure jargon.

Despite (or because of?) the silliness of this term's sound and meaning, it has been used in more than one presidential conversation. In one of Richard Nixon's many White House recordings, H. R. Haldeman makes a very true statement about how BS gets between the public and the government: "To the ordinary guy, all this is a bunch of gobbledygook. But out of the gobbledygook comes a very clear thing: You can't trust the government; you can't believe what they say, and you can't rely on their judgment." Decades later, Ronald Reagan used the word for our ever-impenetrable tax system: "Most [revisions] didn't improve the system; they made it more like Washington itself: complicated, unfair, cluttered with gobbledygook and loopholes designed for those with the power and influence to hire high-priced legal and tax advisers."

President or not, you can make your own gobbledygook at http://www.plainenglish.co.uk/gobbledygook-generator .html, which lays lexical eggs such as "I can make a window to discuss your integrated incremental contingencies" and "Forward-looking companies invest in 21st Century logistical matrix approaches."

gobshite

Do you know anyone who talks a lot of shit? That person is a gobshite, which literally means mouth shit and figuratively means a loudmouth, especially a dumb one.

This mostly Irish word first turns up as a term for a seaman in the U.S. Navy in the early 1900s. By the midtwentieth century it can be found referring to a fool, then a fool with a big mouth. Its 1986 use in John Hockey's *Squaddies: Portrait of a Subculture* is characteristic, as the author describes a sergeant who "was a regular gobshite always shouting at you in barracks."

Another sense of *gob* may have influenced this word: It's been a verb meaning spitting and a noun for a wad of spit. As seen in words like *drivel* and *palaver,* spit is never far from the bullshit lexicon.

This very popular word can be found everywhere from Irish newspapers to the title of literary magazine the *Gobshite Quarterly.* The world is full of gobshites. If we ever run out of them, I'll be gobsmacked.

guff

If you huff and puff, you'll blow a lot of guff.

This term originally referred to a puff or whiff of air, back in the 1800s. That made it a natural addition to the many air-related BS words.

Often guff—as in the common phrase "Don't give me any guff!"—is a type of trouble or protest. A complaining customer is giving guff. A drunken would-be brawler is giving guff. The other key component of guff is that the words are empty, just like the air that originally inspired the word.

An 1889 use from *Sportsman* magazine is true to the word's origins: "He can have the newspapers to him-self, and with that windbag Mitchell fill them with guff and nonsense." That's also a nice play on "stuff and nonsense."

Speaking of rhyme, guff has a lot to do with who's tough. No one considered a hard-ass, badass, or Liam Neeson is likely to take guff.

gurry

Gurry . . . Doesn't sound like anything yummy, does it? And it's not: Gurry is described in an 1859 use from a Bartlett collection of Americanisms as "the slime and blood of fish." Gurry can also include fish oil, blubber, and fish poop. I think I just turned vegetarian.

The word also was used for gunk, dirt, or any kind of mess. A 1949 use from *Harper's* shows the messy sense in use: "The children finally dropped off to sleep, spread amid the gurry on the back seat, like dolls thrown any which way on a rumpled bed."

With those disorderly, gross uses on its résumé, *gurry* was primed for a position in the bullshit lexicon, which it has occupied from time to time in the northeast United States. In Michael Crummey's 2009 novel *River Thieves,* a character refers to "the biggest load of gurry"—that's an emphatic construction often used in calling bullshit.

Or, in this case, fish shit.

hee-haw

This folksy term was originally an imitation of the bray of a donkey. But it can also mean the laughter and blather of a person.

Hee-haw shifted from barnyard asses to human assholes quickly: The fact that this term includes *hee* made for an easy shift to laughter. Such hee-hawing was, like the braying of a donkey, loud and not especially attractive—much like bullshit, which the term also began to cover.

In Australian writer Miles Franklin's novel *All That Swagger* (published in 1936 but written much earlier), the term is used in a way that goes beyond donkeys and laughs: "I met a man out in the Never Never—fellow with a university education—talked real hee-haw like the old parson."

Hee-haw isn't a reduplicative word like *flubdub* and *jibber-jabber*, but it's pretty durn close, and it has the same folksy charm, dagnabbit.

heifer dust

This straight-up euphemism for bullshit is a regional term that, like most euphemisms, is used when protecting the presumably delicate sensibilities of women and tender ears of children.

A 1985 use from *How to Talk Dirty Like Granddad*, by Tom Ladwig, suggests women themselves may prefer the term: "Heifer-dust is what girls say when they mean bullshit." Given the humorous nature of Ladwig's book, this might not be a reliable statement on the girl vocabulary.

Still, like *gentleman cow*, this term is creative and wonderful, showing the wild lengths to which people will go to avoid language that's considered vulgar or gross. It's not common these days, but it's still around. A 2014 article on Tallahassee.com about voting fraud quotes Leon County supervisor of elections Ion Sancho as saying, "It's heifer dust to say that Mickey Mouse can register to vote." Good to know.

Heifer dust can also refer to chewing tobacco, which is the basis for a few BS synonyms around the United States, like *Bull Durham* and *cush*.

hockey

Horse hockey! Bull hockey!

These BS terms would lead you to believe the sport of ice hockey has had a strong influence on the language of bullshit. Perhaps a controversial event—like the bullshit goal that led the Buffalo Sabres to lose the Stanley Cup Finals to the Dallas Stars in 1999—inspired the use of *hockey* in BS terms?

Alas, there is no connection. *Hockey* is simply an old-timey term for excrement. *Hockey*—also spelled *hockie, hocky,* and *hawky*—has been used as a word for dung since at least the late 1800s. It appears related to *cacky,* which brings to mind *caca,* another word for poop.

Any term for excrement is likely to end up in a bullshit euphemism or two. The *Dictionary of American Regional English* records an amusing discussion of the term, which seems to have been used mostly in the southern and midland areas of the United States: "A casual mention of the game called *hockey* will paralyze any Ozark audience, for *hockey* means nothing but dung in the hill country."

hocus-pocus, hokeypokey

Like *abracadabra, hocus-pocus* is a magical form of bullshit—or at least a bullshit word with roots in the sorcerous realm.

Originally the word applied to someone who wasn't a magician or bullshit artist: a juggler. But since juggling was associated with magic, the word was already in the magician's wheelhouse. That's the sense in a 1634 example from *A Relation of Some Yeares Trauaile, Begunne Anno 1626 into Afrique and the Greater Asia.* Thomas Herbert writes about an impressive performer he calls "a Persian Hocus-pocus" who "performed rare tricks with hands and feet." It's easy to imagine such a performer doing a little magic too, and the word drifted in that direction.

From magic and juggling the term spread to trickery and bullshit. By the 1700s you could see sentences like this: "The law is a sort of hocus-pocus science." That oxymoron from Charles Macklin's 1773 novel *Love à la Mode* is an elegant way of calling the law bullshit.

Hocus-pocus also spawned the word *hokeypokey,* which most know as an innocent children's song and dance but which has also been a term for a swindle or bit of nonsense. In J. M. Cain's 1948 novel *The Moth,* when the narrator is accused of caring more about a job than a woman, he responds, "I tell you that's all hokey-pokey."

hogwash

This viscerally satisfying word made a straightforward journey from pigs to people.

Though *hogwash* sounds like something you'd use to clean a pig, there's no pig shampoo in this word's origin story. Instead, one of *wash*'s many early meanings was swill and other unseemly liquids you'd feed to pigs. From there it was a small leap to liquor that wasn't much higher in quality. And from there hogwash became bullshit.

This is one of the more common terms for BS, and it's been so since the 1800s. In *Adventures of Huckleberry Finn,* Mark Twain wrote a sentence that speaks to the power of music and the annoyance of bullshit: "Music is a good thing; and after all that soul-butter and hogwash I never see it freshen things up so." Today Twain might have written, "When life hands you bullshit, listen to some sweet tunes."

Hogwash has been such a successful BS word that even its root, *wash,* came to mean nonsense at times. Georgette Heyer's 1933 novel *Why Shoot a Butler?* mentions "the Public School Spirit, and Playing for the Side, and all that wash." You should appreciate that sentiment if cheerleaders and rah-rah festivities drive you bonkers.

There have also been many variations of *hogwash,* such as *pigswill, pigswash,* and *hogswaddle,* plus the related BS terms *eyewash* and *prop wash.*

One of the most recent variations was coined in the

penultimate episode of *30 Rock* when Jack Donaghy said, "Hogcock!" This obscene-sounding word was actually somewhat innocent, since it was a combination of *hogwash* and *poppycock*.

hokum

It almost rhymes with *bunkum,* but *hokum* is a far more theatrical type of bullshit.

This word began its life as a term for performances that were high on sentiment or melodrama and low on anything else. Hokum—just like our dumbest reality shows, goriest CSI shows, and lamest comedy—appealed to the lowest common denominator. It was crap.

Shakespeare said the world's a stage, and so it's natural that this word for theatrical malarkey proved useful elsewhere. A 1928 use in *Publisher's Weekly* is undoubtedly true, though it might be offensive to the author community: "It is pure hokum to suggest that all authors are always interesting."

Hokum is a very common word that refers to diverse BS. In early 2015 headlines referred to "anti-weed hokum," "political hokum," "art world hokum," and "economic hokum." Unfortunately for us all, there's a lot of hokum to go around.

hooey

Though its origin is uncertain, *hooey* goes back at least as far as 1912. Slang lexicographer Jonathon Green thinks it might be connected to a Russian term for *penis,* the most disreputable organ. There's also a resemblance to the many horse-related words for BS. As with many terms, we may never know the truth from the hooey about *hooey,* which also has the amusing variation *hooey-balooey.*

What isn't uncertain is that hooey is an extremely fun word to say. In *The Female Eunuch,* Germaine Greer used the word memorably while dismissing a bizarre, penis-envy-related explanation for some women's love of horses:

"The horse between a girl's legs is supposed to be a gigantic penis. What hooey!"

Hooey is also a word that's surprisingly presidential. Back in 1948 Harry Truman said, "Daylight saving is a lot of hooey." In 2000 Bill Clinton used it as the conclusion to a trio of bullshit terms describing the media: "I think it's a bunch of bull. . . . I do not think America is very well served by all this rigamarole. . . . That's a bunch of hooey."

Actor, comedian, and writer Bob Odenkirk—most famous for playing Saul Goodman on *Breaking Bad* and *Better Call Saul*—must also dig this word, since he named his 2014 humor collection *A Load of Hooey*.

Hookey Walker (or Walker)

Walker is mainly an exclamation meaning nonsense, horsefeathers, mule fritters, etc. But it started as *Hookey Walker*.

This odd expression is guessed to have come from the name of a ballad, though there's no evidence to support the theory. British lexicographer Michael Quinion notes that there are a few dubious stories of fellas with hooked noses who supposedly inspired the term. We may never know the origin, but we do know the term has been popping up since the early 1800s whenever someone hears something they can't quite believe.

Charles Dickens used this term a few times, including in *A Christmas Carol*. In that novel a wee lad is incredulous that mean ol' Scrooge is being generous. When the boy says "Walk-er!" it's a combination of "Nonsense!" and "Are you for real?" Anytime someone like Scrooge, Montgomery Burns, or Donald Trump does something kind and generous, it's hard not to call bullshit.

In response to BS, you could say "Hookey Walker!" or just "Walker!" But don't bother. Unless you time-travel to London in the 1800s, no one will understand you.

horse apples

Originally a horse apple was simply a type of apple—then it became a term for something that comes out of a horse's bippy and is synonymous with bullshit.

Such terms have been around since the 1600s, and they're still going, at least in rural areas. In this use from Robert Penn Warren's 1955 novel *Band of Angels,* it seems to refer to the dishonest sort of BS: "Maybe now that I got him free of the horse-apple of a lie he had lived with all that time, maybe there wasn't anything to live for now." Obviously, *horse apples* is more likely to be used in a folksy tale than in a statement to the Supreme Court.

You can also call such euphemistic horseshit *horse balls, horse beans, horse biscuits, horse doughnuts, horse dumplings,* or *horse plums.*

horsefeathers

This term—which dates back to the United States in the 1920s—can be understood in two ways.

First, it is a great euphemism for *horseshit:* a word you may not want to use during a first date or a State of the Union speech.

Second, it is a perfect word for nonsense because it *is* nonsense. Until mad scientists create a winged horse like the mythical Pegasus, there will never be horsefeathers. That makes it an apt word to exclaim when someone is trying to sell you a load of rubbish—or a bridge.

Horsefeathers is only the most famous of several related BS terms, such as *bull feathers, gopher feathers,* and—in Australia, naturally—*kangaroo feathers.*

You could probably come up with a new BS word by slapping *feathers* onto any animal—except birds, of course.

horseshit

Is it just me or is *horseshit* even more satisfying to exclaim than *bullshit*?

One of its most powerful uses was in *Step Brothers,* when petulant, immature Brennan Huff (played by Will Ferrell) protests his mother's marriage with the words "This wedding is horseshit!" Ferrell can give any word energy and punch, but *horseshit* is more than halfway there already.

Surprisingly, *horseshit* doesn't appear to be very old. It first turns up in the twentieth century. In a 1925 letter Ernest Hemingway referred to "all this horse shit about Art." William S. Burroughs used it in his classic 1959 novel *Naked Lunch:* "Are we to gulp down this tissue of horse shit?" You can also use the word as a verb: If you horseshit someone, you're trying to put one over on 'em.

If there's ever a bullshit museum, there might have to a whole wing—or stable?—to house all the horse-related words that have been used for BS. Besides *horseshit,* there's *horse apples, horsecock, horse collar, horsecrap, horse dookie, horsefeathers, horse hockey, horse hooey, horse manure, horsepucky,* and *horse radish.*

hot air

Sometimes it feels like hot air is the most abundant gas on earth, what with all the blowhards and bloviators expelling airborne rubbish. This is one of the most literal of BS terms, based on the simple biology of air being expelled while yapping.

Hot air has been used in BS-centric situations since the late 1800s. This 1900 use from George Ade's *Fables in Slang* suggests the term wasn't common: "They strolled under the Maples, and he talked what is technically known as Hot Air."

There are many uses of this term in relation to politicians, and no wonder. When you have to blab and blab over and over—at fund-raisers, debates, town-hall meetings, interviews, etc.—most of what you expel will be gaseous and overwarm.

Such blowhards can be called *hot-air artists* or *hot-air merchants*. There's also the term *hot-air gun*. This is a fanciful weapon possessed by someone with a big mouth. A 1902 use from the *Decatur Herald* mentions a promoter who "knows how to aim his hot air gun."

When your profession is hype and hoopla, you can't afford to bring a knife to a hot-air gunfight.

hubba-hubba

While you may know *hubba-hubba* as mainly a fifties-era word expressing excitement or approval, especially for someone's appearance, it has sometimes meant something other than "Yeah!" or "Ooh-la-la!"

Like other reduplicative words, *hubba-hubba,* which sounds like nonsense, also can mean nonsense.

In Stewart Sterling's 1946 mystery story "Where There's

Smoke," the term appears in this sense: "I suppose you think that's a lot of hubba-hubba." If something's a lot of hubba-hubba, it's a lot of rot, bosh, or tripe.

This word for BS is a little unusual in that its other sense (excitement, approval) is positive. Maybe it was tarnished by sounding too much like *hubbub*.

hubble-bubble

Like *buzz* and *click-clack*, *hubble-bubble* is onomatopoeic.

Originally a hubble-bubble was a type of hookah. From there the term came to mean any bubbling sound—or any verbiage that makes as much sense as a bubbling sound, such as bullshit.

Sometimes a hubble-bubble is a type of jibber-jabber that's just too fast. Other times it can be quite salty and obscene, as in this 1851 use from Thomas Penson De Quincey's essay "Sketch from Childhood": "My brother's wrath had boiled over in such a hubble-bubble of epithets." In other words, "My brother was so freaking angry that he unleashed a shitstorm of swearing." A hubble-bubble is a verbal hubbub.

humblebrag

Many types of bullshit are close to bragging and boasting. Pretending to be humble is also prime bullshit territory. So we should be thankful to the late TV writer and producer Harris Wittels for coining a classic bullshit word.

As Wittels described it on *Grantland:* "A Humblebrag is basically a specific type of bragging which masks the brag in a faux-humble guise. The false humility allows the offender to boast their 'achievements' without any sense of shame or guilt."

Humblebragging is probably as old as false humility and self-aggrandizement, but it has flourished on Twitter, where Wittels retweeted examples, such as:

I just won an ACM, but don't worry I'm still stuck like everyone else in a Taco Bell drive-thru right now.
@cmtcody

Sometimes people I don't even know give me compliments, and I'm just like wtf am I attractive or something?
@RegularOldLuth

Oh dear. Don't know what to do at the airport. Huge crowd, but I'll miss my plane if I stop and do photos...
oh dear don't want to disappoint
@stephenfry

Wittels tapped into a social-media zeitgeist with the term, as #humblebrag became a popular hashtag, @humblebrag exploded in popularity, and the word joined the vernacular. He also wrote *Humblebrag: The Art of False Modesty* in 2012.

humbug

"Bah, humbug!" is the most un-Christmassy expression in English. Before *humbug* was used to call bullshit on December 25, it had a long history, mostly on the criminal side of the tracks.

Since at least the mid-1700s, a humbug has been a hoax or other type of trickery, sometimes intended to steal your money, other times intended to tickle your fancy. The word originally had a strong association with jesters and clowns. It could also be used for anything that's not what it appears to be. A married man pretending to be single? Humbug! A politician's lies? Humbug! An urban legend? Humbug! Then as now, there was no lack of humbug.

You could also say you humbugged someone—or engaged in the amusing-sounding practice of humbuggism or humbuggery. An 1892 use from *The Voice* shows an understandable cynicism about politics: "Hypocrisy and humbuggery are openly declared to be the only traits that entitle a man to political support."

If only politicians were allowed to be honest. It would be refreshing to see the slogan "Hypocrisy and Humbuggery in 2016."

jabber, jibber, jibber-jabber

Jabbering is yakking: chattering and blabbing quickly and without any sense at all. These days it seems someone is always jabbering on their phone when you're trying to concentrate.

Jabber is often used for any kind of lingo or language you don't understand. In *Gulliver's Travels,* Jonathan Swift mentioned people "who only differ from their Brother Brutes in Houyhnhnmland, because they use a Sort of Jabber." As with most forms of bullshit, it's always other people who jabber.

Jabber and *jibber* have been surpassed in the lexicon by their reduplicative offspring *jibber-jabber* (also spelled *jibba-jabba*). On *The A-Team* Mr. T was famous for denouncing two things: fools and jibba-jabba.

But like so many words spread by TV, *jibber-jabber* had been around for a while. Mr. T would likely nod his head approvingly at this 1948 use from the *Philadelphia Bulletin:* "Time for Congress to quit jibber-jabbering."

Jackson Pollock, Niagara Falls

Many people have probably looked at Jackson Pollock's artwork—in all its paint-splattering, abstract glory—and thought, "That's bullshit." Some may feel that Niagara Falls is like a leaky faucet compared to the Grand Canyon, and therefore bullshit.

However, there's a simpler explanation for why these terms are in the bullshit lexicon: You can blame Cockney rhyming slang. *Niagara Falls* rhymes with *balls,* and *Jackson Pollock* rhymes with *bollock.* So just as *apples and pears* means *stairs,* these names took on new meanings—for testicles and nonsense.

Whether a load of Niagara Falls is more bullshit than a bunch of Jackson Pollocks is hard to say.

jargon

Alas, poor *jargon*! Though this word has a respectable meaning—the language of a profession or field—it has another, more common meaning: BS. People generally have as much respect for jargon as for horsepucky.

Jargon has had a long life as a word with many shifts in meaning. Its first known sense didn't apply to people at all: It was the twittering of birds or the sounds of other animals. That meaning is rare today but has been around since the 1300s, and in 1830 poet Henry Wadsworth Longfellow used it: "With beast and bird the forest rings / Each in his jargon cries or sings."

From there *jargon* came to mean nonsense or gibberish, but these days it most often applies to corporate bullshit. One of the best-ever spoofs of this painful variety of English was "synergizing backwards overflow," a phrase used by Jack Donaghy on *30 Rock.* If you've ever had to reach out to a stakeholder about silos or verticals, you've waded through this type of bullshit.

jazz

Jazz music might be the great American invention. But the word *jazz* doesn't always have such a lofty, respectable meaning.

The origins of this word are not clear, but several meanings emerged around the same time in the 1920s. Besides the music, *jazz* meant energy or vigor. It also meant rubbish or unnecessary blather. You could easily substitute *bullshit* for *jazz* in this 1917 use from the *Milwaukee Journal:* "You meet a young lady and tell her how extremely well she is looking. . . . Then she responds: 'Jazz, old fellow, pure jazz! Shut it off and talk regular.'"

The sense of *jazz* as BS might have something to do with a baseball meaning: *Jazz* can refer to a pitch so tricky and unpredictable it's almost impossible to hit. That sense is used here in a *Los Angeles Times* article from 1912: "Ben's Jazz Curve . . . 'I got a new curve this year. . . . I call it the Jazz ball because it wobbles and you simply can't do anything with it.'"

To a hitter such a baffling pitch surely seems like bullshit.

kibosh

This word—commonly but inconclusively believed to be Yiddish in origin—is usually used when talking about ending something. If you put the kibosh on a plan, you rejected the plan. When something is kiboshed, it's finished.

Perhaps that end result—nothingness—led this to be an occasional term for nonsense in the later 1800s. This 1885 use from *Punch* has a BS-ish sense: "Still I wish you a 'Appy New Year, if you care for the kibosh, old Chappie." Today you might say, "Happy New Year, dude, if you're into that kind of tommyrot."

It's also possible that sense was influenced by a common word for BS: *bosh.*

After all, people make meaning with their ears just as often as their dictionaries. If a word sounds like nonsense, it probably will be used that way. Just as *kabillion* sounds like some indefinite number bigger than a billion, *kibosh* kind of sounds like a larger-than-usual bunch of bosh.

lunch meat

Few foodies will swoon over the word *lunch meat,* which conjures images, smells, and tastes of the most rubbishy meat imaginable—which is probably why it's sometimes been used as a term for bullshit.

The most famous person to use the term is not a person at all: Sitcom character Alf, in the episode "Hail to the Chief," said "Aw, lunchmeat!" in response to a jargon-filled description of an environmental plan.

Lunch meat is a euphemism for another common word for bullshit: *baloney.*

macaroni

Though best known as a type of noodle—and sometimes used as an insult for a dandy, which is the sense used in "Yankee Doodle"—*macaroni* is also a type of nonsense.

This sense was given to *macaroni* from a variation: *macaronic*. That adjective refers to a jumble, especially a lexical jumble. In macaronic poetry, words from different languages are used together. Originally words from other tongues were inserted into Latin with Latin inflections. Today it can involve any kind of mixed-language poetry, such as the following terrible poem:

> *Yo quiero una hamburgesa*
> *I am quite parched*
> *Also my shirt is a bit overstached*
> *Tu madre es francesca*

That type of lexical mishmash led to *macaroni*'s taking on this mixy meaning, which eventually brought the word to mean nonsense and bullshit. In Josef von Sternberg's 1965 autobiography *Fun in a Chinese Laundry,* you can feel the weariness that's common when dealing with BS: "What is flashed from the projector overhead will be the same old macaroni."

This meaning has no relation whatsoever to the macaroni penguin, which is quite adorable and non-bullshit-spewing.

madam

This is an old—and old-fashioned—title for a woman. *Madam* feels a little like bullshit today, which is fitting given one of its senses.

Madam had been used in mostly respectful ways starting in the 1300s, but by the 1500s the term had shifted in the opposite direction. Much as you can use *princess* to describe a woman who's full of herself, *madam* was beginning to be used in insulting and ironic ways. The term was used for young girls who were conceited and young women who were considered hussies. The biggest shift was the prostitution-centric meaning: *Madam* started referring to a female pimp starting in the late 1800s.

Since brothels have long been known as a good place to get robbed, that might be how *madam* hooked its way into the language of humbuggery. In some cases *madam* was simply flattery, but it could be virtually any form of nonsense. The phrase often used was "the usual madam." These days the usual madam is likely to involve some jackass stealing your credit card number.

The horseshitty sense of *madam* shows up in John Wainwright's 1972 novel *A Touch of Malice:* "It was not the sort of place conducive to putting over a spot of old madam." In other words, it was the rarest of rarities: an actual no-bullshit zone.

malarkey

This is one of the most popular words for bullshit, and it's easy to see why; 93.5 percent of the population is unable to resist smiling after saying or hearing it.

As lexicographer Ben Zimmer has noted, cartoonist Thomas Aloysius Dorgan was a popularizer of this Irish American word, which has an unknown origin. Some think it started as a last name, but that's just conjecture. It did appear with a few different spellings, such as *milarkey* and *malachy,* in the early part of the twentieth century. This 1924 example from the *Indiana Evening Gazette* is the *Oxford English Dictionary*'s earliest: "The rest of the chatter is so much malarkey, according to a tip so straight that it can be passed thru a peashooter without touching the sides." That meant roughly: "I heard extremely credible information, and the rest is gossip and horseshit."

Though *malarkey* is a bit old-fashioned, it isn't rare these days, and it has a patron saint: Joe Biden. As Barack Obama's vice president, Biden has become highly associated with this word. He made headlines when he used it in an October 2012 debate against Paul Ryan, saying, "With all due respect, that's a bunch of malarkey." That's an expression he's used other times, including in early 2015 when he discussed an economic uptick: "Mark my words, the Republican Party is going to try to claim this resurgence. . . . It's a bunch of malarkey." For politicians, who hear and spew so much bullshit, it must be nice to have a synonym that's family-friendly.

Malarkey has also inspired a rare variation: *arkymalarkey*. That appears to be a word beloved, and perhaps invented, by Carl Sandburg, who used it a few times to mean bullshit in the 1930s and '40s. Slang-meister Jonathon Green thinks *arkymalarkey* might be related to *ackamarackus*, another silly-sounding, ultrafun BS word.

mansplain

Though mansplaining is likely as old as condescending cavemen, the word itself is a recent addition to the lexicon of bullshit. An Urban Dictionary definition from 2009 (around the time of its emergence) sums it up: "To explain in a patronizing manner, assuming total ignorance on the part of those listening. The mansplainer is often shocked and hurt when their mansplaination is not taken as absolute fact, criticized or even rejected altogether."

The worst type of mansplaining is likely when a man— often a politician—explains women's issues to women as if he were the foremost lady expert in the world. This word can also cover the male tendency to drone on about anything like an expert, regardless of actual knowledge or audience interest. Whether in a bar or on cable TV, when some blowhard is letting you know how it really is, that's mansplaining.

The word *mansplaining* has been so successful that the suffix *-splain* has become successful on its own. Like the suffix *-iness* in *truthiness, -splain* is shorthand for a type of bullshit, particularly bullshit of a patronizing sort.

For example, *ablesplainers* are nondisabled people telling disabled people what disability is all about. *Cisplainers* are nontransgendered people speaking for (or to) the transgendered community. People use the *-splain* suffix when someone is talking out of their ass.

Even superheroes aren't immune. In 2010's *Batman and Robin* #18, villainess Una Nemo accused the caped crusader of mansplaining, which led a blogger to coin *Batsplain*. If you imagine Batsplaining in Christian Bale's voice, it's 60 percent funnier.

You can also *gaysplain, journosplain, babysplain,* and *grammarsplain*. A classic grammarsplanation would be correcting a grammatical error with a statement that includes a new goof.

Not all these meanings are as obnoxious as the original *mansplain*. Many writers now use the suffix for humorous effect, like Megan Garber in the *Atlantic:* "Today in *shoesplaining:* Until your career is at its height, ladies, maybe you should stick to flats."

I could tell you more about mansplaining if you have four to five hours free, ladies.

meadow muffins, meadow mayonnaise

The alliterative term *meadow muffins* has a ring to it. A disgusting ring, but a ring.

The barnyard—which is, after all, the home of actual bovine poopy—is never far from the bullshit lexicon. One of many euphemisms for literal bullshit is *meadow muffins,* which can refer to the droppings of many animals. Muffinologists like slang lexicographer Jonathon Green have noted the variations *meadow cake* and *trail muffins.*

In Celeste Palermo's 2009 book *The Coffee Mom's Devotional: A Rich Blend of 30 Brief and Inspiring Devotions,* the word is used in a nonbarnyard sense: "I'd like to say that I'm ambitious and enterprising and that cerebral rats thrive in creative environments, but that is a self-deluded pile of meadow muffins."

A close relative is *meadow mayonnaise* (or *meadow dressing*). This is a twentieth-century term used in the United States and Australia, and the condiment aspect is key. Meadow mayo isn't the kind of bullshit that just sits there. It's not the kind you dump on someone in a think piece or holiday letter. Rather, meadow mayonnaise is the kind of bullshit you spread around, covering everything and everyone in a thick coating of BS.

Spread the word.

meshugas

This Yiddish word mainly means "Madness!" As seen in words like *batshit* and *nuts, madness* is very close to nonsense, foolishness, and bullshit.

This 1965 use from Chaim Bermant's novel *Ben Preserve Us* is very much in tune with *psychobabble:* "It isn't medicine really, psychiatry, it's a *meschugas,* and very profitable." This is a colorful way of saying psychiatry is based on bunk and greed more than on facts and science.

The word is used more generally in this 1993 example from *Toronto Life:* "He now owns a three-bedroom house at the Fountains of Palm Beach, a good couple of hours' drive from the meshugges of Miami Beach."

That sounds like a safe distance from Miami Beach and its bullshit.

Mickey Mouse

Since this alliterative rodent first appeared in 1928's *Steamboat Willie,* he's been one of the most popular Disney characters. Within a few years his name was being taken in vain, or at least in figurative senses that related to insignificant pip-squeaks and, oddly, a doohickey in a plane that releases bombs. More commonly, anything described as Mickey Mouse was unimportant or small-time.

But *Mickey Mouse* can also mean mouse shit—or rather,

bullshit. This especially applies to activities considered pointless, and the term has turned up on several surveys of college slang. Students from many time periods could relate to a definition from a 1963 *American Speech* article: "An assignment which is regarded as foolish and a waste of time is a *Mickey Mouse.*" Decades later, slang guru Jonathan Lighter recorded a 1993 example from CNN's *NewsHour* of the phrase "a load of Mickey Mouse."

Presumably a small load. Mickey Mouse is bullshit that would barely stick to your shoe.

moody

Though today we mostly know this word as an adjective for someone who's a bit emotional, it has another meaning that's less about feelings and more about flimflam.

This British term emerged in the 1930s as similar to the original meaning of *humbug:* a method of trickery or deceit. The first known use is from Philip Allingham's 1934 novel *Cheapjack,* which gives insight into how it was used: "When they [a mark] did not believe something you were saying they would tell you to 'cut out the moody.'" The moody could entail mere flattery or a more complicated scheme to separate innocent dupes from their cash.

This term evolved from criminal chicanery to general horseshit. In 1975 P. G. Winslow's *Death of an Angel* used the word in way that's synonymous with bullshit: "He'd been talking big . . . all a lot of moody."

Whether it means criminal activity or common crapola, you can't trust a lot of moody.

moonshine

Sometimes a word's history is deceiving. You likely know the type of moonshine that's homemade liquor. You might think *moonshine* became a word for BS due to the uncertain composition of such illicit, DIY happy juice. After all, quality control is tough to maintain in a bathtub.

But *moonshine* as nonsense is much older than the moonshine you drink out of a jug. This first appeared as a word for nonsense in the idiom "moonshine in the water," which refers to any nebulous stuff that's not real. Moonshine isn't material: It might look pretty, but if you try to grab it, you'll have no luck. A bunch of moonshine is a bunch of nothing.

A rare expression from the 1500s—"to hang by the moonshine"—refers to things that are completely made up. If your Facebook post or Nobel Prize acceptance speech hangs by the moonshine, it lacks facts. You must've been drinking moonshine when you wrote it.

mouthwash

For many people mouthwash is an essential part of dental hygiene, not to mention a good idea before a date. For others it's just bullshit—literally.

Actual mouthwash has existed since the 1800s, and by the 1900s the term was established enough that it could be a metaphor. Fiction writer C. S. Lewis suggested in a 1957 letter that reading the *Odyssey* would "give your imagination a good mouth-wash."

In the 1900s the word became a term for bull, as shown in this 1971 use from a legal journal: "Any suggestion that the principle was also applied can be dismissed as so much mouth-wash." In the land of legal mumbo jumbo, you can never have enough words for bullshit.

Probably the shift to BS was influenced by the successful term *hogwash,* which also influenced *belly wash* and *prop wash.*

mule fritters

Few language items are more enjoyable than an exclamation meaning, roughly, "That's a load of bullshit!" One TV character in particular was known for such exclamations, which he produced by the boatload: *M*A*S*H*'s Colonel Potter.

"Mule fritters!"—a straight-up synonym for bullshit—is a classic, but Potter used many similar terms. Some were already in use, and some seem to have been coined for the show.

Much like the invented BS exclamations of *Futurama*—like *crapspackle* and *drivel-poop*—Potterisms tended to play on established BS terms. For example, *pig feathers* is a play on *horsefeathers*. *Pony pucks* is similar to *horsepucky* and *bull-pucky*. *Pigeon pellets* is like ... I'm not sure what that's like. It's pure, exclamatory poetry, of which Potter produced a bunch, including:

> Buffalo chips!
> Hot sausage!
> Crock of beans!
> Cow cookies!
> Beaver biscuits!

Colonel Potter is a great reminder that even with hundreds of BS words in the world, there is always room for another. Perhaps yesterday's *mule fritters* will inspire tomorrow's *labradoodle cronuts*.

mullock

Though *mullock* has meant rubbish as far back as the 1300s, a meaning that emerged in the 1800s is equally relevant and more interesting. *Mullock* was rock, but rock that was missing something: gold. It could also mean the rubble and refuse left after gold was extracted.

In any era a lack of gold is considered absolute, unadulterated bullshit, and that's where this word drifted next.

This meaning emerged in the mid-1800s, not long after the advent of the gold-free meaning. In Hal Porter's 1965 short-story collection *The Cats of Venice,* there's a question that's still popular over breakfast: "What mullock has been unloaded on us this fair morn?"

Mullock—which sounds like the child of *malarkey* and *bollocks*—contains a perfect metaphor for bullshit. When you're looking for gold in a book, article, speech, or explanation, nothing's more disappointing than mullock.

mumbo jumbo

This is probably the most successful of all the reduplicative words for bullshit, and we know its origin in more detail than most.

Mumbo jumbo originally had a religious sense: It was applied to a West African god in the 1700s. From there *mumbo jumbo* spread to mean other types of superstitious, spiritual, or religious matters. At first the term conveyed a sense of awe. In the following use from the *Atlantic Monthly* in 1892, making a mumbo jumbo of something would involve giving it respect and power: "He does not undervalue the use of party, but he refuses to surrender his principles to party, or to make a Mumbo Jumbo of it."

Since all beliefs, religious or not, are BS to nonbelievers, the term also took on a diminishing meaning that it still has today. *Mumbo jumbo* became a bunch of gibberish or nonsense. These days it can refer to almost any kind of BS, from a politician's empty promises to a manual's indecipherable jargon.

Speaking of politics and jargon, a *Time* article from early 2015 on an attempt by the U.S. government to streamline its language has a headline that, appropriately, is quite clear: "Government Officials May Be Using Less Mumbo Jumbo."

newspeak

Some BS words have a more literary pedigree than others, and that's certainly true of this word coined by George Orwell in his famous dystopian novel *1984*, published in 1949.

Newspeak isn't quite a language: It is a group of mostly compound terms such as *goodsex* and *crimethink*. Their overall purpose is control: That's why *newspeak* caught on as a term for language that seems determined to stifle thought rather than convey it.

Nowadays any kind of baffling or coercive language

used by politicians or the media could be labeled *newspeak*, particularly euphemisms. In *Counterpunch*, Abby Martin discusses vile terms such as *mowing the lawn* (mowing down civilians) and other revolting uses of language: "Disturbing Newspeak phrases that absolve their pillaging and mass murder have permeated society and warped our interpretation of reality." That's the essence of newspeak: thought control.

This word launched the suffix *-speak*, which can be found in words such as *management-speak, teacher-speak,* and *parent-speak*.

It's a tough world. Even if you elude Big Brother, there's no escape from Big Bullshit.

nitshit

If you think *batshit* is as low as it goes in the metaphorical feces department, there's also *nitshit*, which refers to the dookie of a louse. That makes even dog shit or frog shit seem like a big deal.

Since the 1970s this has been a U.S. term for extremely trivial nonsense, and it's one of the most appropriate in the lexicon. Nits and bullshit are both annoying and unwanted, so *nitshit* is a fitting term for unnecessary trivialities.

This seems like a particularly useful term when putting things in perspective, since *nitshit* is ideal for describing the nonsense that's a tiny turd, not a massive mound. For example:

Bullshit: Losing your house.

Nitshit: Losing the loyalty card an annoying coffee chain talked you into signing up for just to get a free coffee.

Bullshit: The national government.

Nitshit: The local government.

Bullshit: Marrying a terrible person.

Nitshit: Eating a terrible sandwich.

nuts, nertz

Much like *balls* and *bollocks, nuts* is a testicular term used to call bullshit on something. People say "Nuts!" when they can't believe what they're hearing.

This meaning dates from the early 1900s, and it's also common to see "Nuts to that!" and "Nuts to you!" The latter is more of a general insult, while the former is close to "That's bullshit!"

There's also *nertz* (or *nerts*). This playful spelling of *nuts* has been around since at least 1931 as a way to say something is nonsense. The following statements and replies would all be logical, if not appropriate:

> All my music explores the innermost depths of my
> soul.
> *Nertz!*
> Let's touch base after I run this up the flagpole.
> *Nertz!*
> Vote for me and I'll put your interests ahead of big
> corporations.
> *Nertz!*

Like *nuts,* you can find *nertz* being used to mean crazy and testicles.

A 2014 *Los Angeles Times* book review of *A Master Builder* by Michael Phillips offers this comment: "You believe the relationships even when the behavior and the psychology is frankly nertz."

Nertz is also a super-fast card game that involves shouting "Nertz!"—not because of bullshit but because you've laid down all your cards.

oil

There are plenty of liquids that do language a solid by naming bullshit. So why not oil?

Just as oil makes an engine run smoothly, another kind of oil is a conversational lubricant—often one not to be trusted.

The *Oxford English Dictionary*'s earliest example with this meaning, from 1917 in *American Magazine,* shows how suspect oil can be: "'Why dearie!' I remarks, kissin' her; 'You know I—'. 'Easy with the oil!' she cuts me off." In other words, "Easy on the flummery, buddy! I don't kiss bullshitters."

okey-doke

If any type of BS is okay, it has to be *okey-doke,* which started as an alternative version of *okay* (along with *okey-dokey*) in the 1930s.

By the 1960s *okey-doke* had started to take on a meaning very close to bullshit: a type of swindle or con job. In the same decade the word also started to refer to foolishness and nonsense, putting it squarely in the bullshit spectrum.

A 1992 use in Terry McMillan's *Waiting to Exhale* shows the bullshit sense is still influenced by the scam sense: "Why did I allow myself to fall for the okeydoke and do this shit?" In other words, "I fell for some real mumbo jumbo and ended up doing some fiddle-faddle."

Be sure not to fall for the okey-doke or—worse—the old okey-doke, which sounds 67.3 percent scammier.

paff

Is it just me, or are the one-syllable bullshit words the most fun to say? Bosh! Rot! Balls!

Paff!

Words like *paff* are perfect for dismissing nonsense that doesn't deserve more than one breath or syllable of rebuttal.

This term had an explosive origin: as a sound effect similar to "Bam!" and "Pow!" The first recorded use, in Charles Smith's 1800 comedy *The Wild Youth*—includes a few similar words: "I shall fire alarm guns—Piff! Paff! Puff!" *Paff* could indicate an explosion, a gunshot, or a punch.

Since *paff* was already a close associate of the exclamation mark, it was a natural word to use in exclamations proclaiming nonsense. This sense emerged in the later 1800s, and it was used in James Joyce's *Ulysses* in 1922: "What offence laid fire to their brains? Paff!"

Often *paff* is used with the similar-sounding *piff*, as here in a 2002 *Daily Telegraph* article: "Let the BBC do its worst! I say pif! paf! to their devil's box of tricks! We shall never surrender!"

It doesn't hurt that *piff* is part of *piffle*, another BS word.

palaver

If you've ever tried to argue with someone on the Internet, you've waded into some deep bullshit—and it was probably quite a *palaver*, a term with an argument-centric origin.

Palaver was originally a West African word for some type of official or legal dispute, dating back to the early 1700s. From there it came to mean just about any kind of fuss or trouble, and it was often used in combination with other terms. For example, you could have war palaver, woman palaver, or even tummy palaver. The word could also stand for someone's concern or business, as in "That's none of your palaver!"

Along the way the term took on a few meanings related to bullshit: flattery and blabbing. In the United States the term came to also refer to an extremely popular form of bullshit: jargon. No less than the great Mark Twain used the term in this sense. In 1909's *Is Shakespeare Dead?* Twain writes, "I have been a quartz miner in the silver regions—a pretty hard life; I know all the palaver of that business." I'd say "the palaver of a business" is damn near a perfect definition of jargon.

This term has also inspired a few words for bullshitters, like *palaverist* and *palaverer*.

panther piss

Warning: This term has no relation to Sex Panther, the cologne that "smells like pure gasoline" yet is still preferred by Brian Fantana in *Anchorman: The Legend of Ron Burgundy.*

But panther piss was originally another type of liquid found in small containers and sometimes compared to gasoline: strong liquor.

A 1929 article from linguistics journal *American Speech* on "Wet Words in Kansas" recorded this term along with other animalistic terms for strong drinks preferred by serious alcohol enthusiasts. If panther piss wasn't your thing, you might have enjoyed monkey-swill or rat-track whiskey. For panther lovers there was also panther blood and panther sweat.

Since these terms were not generally compliments for the beverages in question, some came to mean BS (since the 1950s). For example, in the 1986 film *Heartbreak Ridge,* Tom Highway says of himself, "It seems that marriage and the Marine Corps weren't too compatible." Mary Jackson, the widow of one of Tom's buddies, refutes that notion: "Panther piss. The best years of my life were spent with a marine. If I were a little younger, I'd make you eat your words and curl your toes."

That meaning is charming but rare, though *panther piss* lives on in the world of alcohol. On DrinksMixer.com there's a recipe for Panther Piss, which contains white rum, triple sec, lime juice, and Sprite—but no horse apples.

pants

Load of crap! Bunch of balderdash! Pile of pants!

Pile of pants?

While a pile of dirty pants can be a smelly, disgusting biohazard, that's not the image that inspired the idiom. As British etymologist Michael Quinion points out, his countrymen refer to underpants as *pants,* so this term is meant to suggest tighty-whities rather than trousers.

The most common form seems to be the alliterative phrase "pile of pants," which can be seen in a 1996 article from *Sporting Life:* "Snooker? I'd rather we never won a medal of any sort again than see that pile of pants being accorded Olympic status."

One can also say something is "complete pants" or "absolute pants" if it's rubbish.

A 2000 use from London's *Independent* newspaper puts the word in a realm that is overflowing with pants, politics: "A Liberal Democrat stunned his fellow peers when he dismissed a landmark report on the future of the historic environment as 'a load of pants'."

When it comes to the bullshit lexicon, a load of pants is a lot more (and less) than laundry.

pedlar's French

Pedlar—a variation of *peddler*—is a word with a tangled history involving many forms of bullshit.

It started as a term for a trader, particularly one who went door to door. That meaning's been around since the 1300s, and I assume such pedlars were as annoying then as they are today.

By the 1530s English folks were using *pedlar's French* for criminal cant: their own in-group language, similar to slang or jargon. Since pedlar's French made no sense to most people—it was a coded language understood only by criminals—it came to be used as a term for any stuff that made no sense. The 1699 *New Dictionary of the Terms Ancient and Modern of the Canting Crew* describes the term as "a sort of Gibrish" and lumps it with beggars and Gypsies for a double whammy of disparagement and racism.

This is a pretty common journey for a word for nonsense. The train of thought seems to be: "I don't understand this. Therefore, it is nonsense. Now I will use its name for all nonsense and bullshit." This progression can be seen when *Greek* or *Dutch* is used to mean nonsense.

Another meaning of *pedlar* may have had an influence on its migration to the bullshit lexicon: A pedlar was also a gossip.

philosophunculist

Appearances aside, this word does not refer to a very punctual philosopher or an expert in the philosophy of punctuation. It simply is, as the *Oxford English Dictionary* puts it, "a petty or insignificant philosopher."

Philosophy doesn't get a lot of respect anyway: Think of all the jokes about how getting a philosophy degree leads straight to the poorhouse. So a word for a small-time philosopher is especially disparaging. It's like a bullshit artist with two MFAs.

In *Stranger in a Strange Land* sci-fi writer Robert A. Heinlein uses the term humorously: "You know, or should know, that I am a senior philosophunculist on active duty."

That's like being a tenured professor of balderdash at Bunk University.

phooey

"Phooey!" was first a way to express disapproval or say no to something. The first known use was in 1919 in a caption appearing in the *Sandusky (Ohio) Star-Journal:* "Phooey! That's old stuff—she told me pers'n'ly that all of them 'sweet patootie' letters was forged."

An example from J. B. Priestley's 1951 novel *Festival at Farbridge* shows its disapproving power in action: "Oh phooey, Benny. . . . This don't count as a drink." You would never hear someone say or write, "Phooey! This is exactly what I wanted."

From there a tiny shift in meaning brought *phooey* from disapproval to nonsense and bullshit. Famed fiction writer Raymond Chandler used the term in a 1946 letter: "So let's not have any more of that phooey about 'as literature my stuff still stinks.'"

Sounds like Chandler was calling someone out on a humblebrag long before Harris Wittels coined the term.

pickles

Pickles has been on the bullshit spectrum since the 1800s. It was common back then to say of something ridiculous or absurd that it was "all pickles."

A 2004 use from the *Orange County Register* shows the term hasn't gone away: "In times of extreme exasperation, she would fume, 'Oh, fiddlesticks!' or, if she was really provoked, 'Oh, pickles!'"

There are certainly less logical words for bullshit, which—like a pickle—can leave a sour taste in the mouth.

piddle

Here's another BS word that, like *doo-doo,* comes to us from the kindergarten bathroom: *piddle.* Piddle is pee—or, if you're putting on airs, urine.

Piddle can be a noun or a verb, and it's had this urinary meaning since the late 1800s. Since urine is not exactly a bourbon barrel–aged stout, it doesn't inspire a lot of respect. That disrespect for pee—already inherent in a childish word like *piddle*—made this a natural term for anything trivial or nonsensical.

English poet and member of the Bloomsbury group Rupert Brooke gave this advice in 1910: "It's the alteration of the little words that makes all the difference between Poetry & piddle."

Indeed. And words don't get any littler (in meaning anyway) than *piddle.*

piffle

This term brings to mind *piff* and *paff,* and it's reminiscent of *trifle,* which is fitting. A piffle sounds like a whole lot of nothing, which is exactly what it is: a small, insubstantial type of BS—the kind you'd wave away with your hand.

The first known use, from the London *Saturday Review* in 1890, mentions "a certain amount of the 'piffle' (to use a University phrase) thought to be incumbent on earnest young princes in our century." It makes sense that royalty would be fond of piffles. Even today the likes of the British royal family aren't exactly known for cutting-edge medical research or saving babies from burning buildings. Their whole lives can seem a piffle: a bunch of silly nonsense.

An early 2015 opinion column in *Bernews* by Larry Burchall uses the expression "political piffle and waffle"—a memorable turn of phrase with a bit of redundancy. *Political* is practically synonymous with *piffle* and *waffle* already.

pillowcase

This is a word for a bullshitter. Or maybe I should say a horseshitter, since this term has a connection to the large family of words that includes *horsepucky* and *horse apples*.

In 1922 an article in the *Edwardsville (Illinois) Intelligencer* called "The Flapper's Dictionary" gave this definition: "Pillow Case: Young man who is full of feathers." But not just any feathers: horsefeathers, aka horseshit.

This term is rare and obscure, but it is evidence of something: There is so much bullshit in the world that just about any word could potentially be used to name it.

The exclamation "Pillow pigeons!" sounds like another term for BS, but it's not. Pillow pigeons are bedbugs.

pish, pish-posh, posh

All three permutations of this word can mean bullshit: "Pish!" and "Posh!" and "Pish-posh!"

More than any other sound, *sh* is linked with bullshit. *Bosh* and *tosh* are words for bullshit, and of course you can't spell *shit* without *sh*. The *sh* sounds add to the bullshit-tastic sound of *pish-posh* and its components.

First there was *pish*. Early uses are reduplicated and express contempt, as in Thomas Nashe's 1592 *Pierce Penilesse:* "Pish, pish, what talke you of olde age or balde pates." Today you might say, "Oh horseshit, what do you know about being a geezer and a cue ball?"

Where there's contempt there's often bullshit, and *pish* shifted in meaning to be not only a response to bullshit but also a synonym for it. Saul Bellow used that sense in 1944's *Dangling Man:* "This is pish, nonsense, nothing!" A 2003 use in *Snoop* contains a memorable bit of scientific journalism: "A psychologist claims that a group of lesbian monkeys shows that Darwin's theories of evolution are pish."

The similar-sounding *posh* also became a word for nonsense in the twentieth century to go along with *bosh* and *tosh*. And when you put *pish* and *posh* together, you get *pish-posh*. There's also *pishery-pashery:* yet another dismissive term that shows rhyme and bullshit go together like big butts and Sir Mix-A-Lot.

pony

We all know ponies as little horses. But a pony can also be a little horseshit.

That meaning has been around since the 1930s, when George Orwell recorded the word as meaning "a shit" in 1931. This 1986 use—from Tom Barling's crime novel *The Smoke*—is a sentiment we can all agree with: "I just don't want to be face down in pony knowing you'll end up smelling of violets." The word also turns up in familiar BS constructions like "all that old pony" and "a load of old pony," showing that the word, like so many others, has moved from literal to figurative crap.

In England you can still find this term from time to time. For example, in a 2013 article from London's *Telegraph,* Katy Brand writes about a scandal over the real ingredients of the Findus Crispy Pancake, "The Findus website stated that they 'only use the best ingredients along with a pinch of imagination', and now we know what that 'pinch of imagination' is: a load of pony."

Mmm, pony pancakes.

poppycock

Poppycock combines a childish sound with a hard final consonant to make a word built to reduce any argument to dust (not necessarily donkey dust). And the origin of *poppycock* makes it even more enjoyable.

The word comes from *poppekak,* a Dutch word that appears only in the idiom *zo fijn als gemalen poppekak.* Figuratively that means someone is a little overzealous in the religious department. Literally it means "fine as powdered doll excrement." So poppycock is doll poop. That might even be lowlier than nitshit.

Despite its old-fashioned sound—or maybe because of it—this is still a popular word. In late 2014 and early 2015 publications included references to "smarmy poppycock," "idealistic poppycock," "judgmental poppycock," "pure poppycock," and "liberal poppycock." Some headline writer had fun with this one about NBC's woes: "More Poppycock from Peacock Network."

Since dolls don't poop (outside of a dream I'd like to forget), *poppycock* is a perfect word for BS. Poppycock is so suspect, it's not even real poop. At least horseshit and batshit are real.

There's also *cockypop:* an inverted synonym associated with actor/comedian Foster Brooks.

poppy-show

Poppycock isn't the only puppet-related BS word.

As far back as the 1600s *poppy-show* was an alternate word for a puppet show or other type of tiny performance. By the 1800s *poppy-show* had shifted in meaning to include not just a literal performance but any kind of showy, ostentatious display—like the kind of performance people put on when shoveling BS. This word is particularly common in the Caribbean.

This 1994 use in Patricia Powell's novel *A Small Gathering of Bones* shows that the word can identify a friend who is all show and no go: "Ian's poppy-show friends never around when him need them."

A poppy-show friend, like a fair-weather friend, is pretty much a bullshit friend.

prattle

"Cease your prattle!" That's a rather old-fashioned way to say "Shut yer pie-hole!"

Prattle emerged in the 1500s as a word for blabbering that is, as the *Oxford English Dictionary* puts it, "idle, garrulous, or childish." The word made an unusual shift in the next few centuries, moving away from yap-happy people. Many BS words start off with some kind of non-BS meaning, but this one made the opposite journey, traveling from the words of people to the sounds produced by animals and things, as long as they were also meaningless. From the 1700s on, you could refer to the prattling of a blackbird, fountain, or bunch of leaves à la "babbling brook." Though *prattle* shifted in meaning, it continued to refer to human yakety-yak.

Just as prattling is rambling on, often with gossip and other dubious information, *prattle-prattle* is insubstantial or foolish stuff. You can also refer to a chronic prattler as a *prattle-box* or *prattle-basket,* and a bunch of prattling as *prattlement.*

prop wash

Another member of the *wash* family of BS words is *prop wash.* This is probably one of the least colorful terms contributed by the military, which has been an unparalleled breeding ground for filth and obscenity, particularly when it comes to F-word variations.

The literal sense of this Air Force slang term is air or water sent flying by a propeller. If that air or water hits you in the face, you've got an eyeful (or even grosser, a mouthful) of prop wash. So prop wash was unpleasant from the start.

However, that uncomfortable situation might be preferable to the figurative sense, which is hogwash, nonsense, crapola. A 1963 use from the *Optometric Weekly* about the definition of *boat* takes this Air Force term out to sea: "At the risk of rousing the ire of former Navy men, we maintain that their fetish that *boat* cannot be applied to a seagoing vessel is all prop-wash." When it comes to word use and history, it's often tough to tell good sense from prop wash.

prune juice

Prune juice isn't without its merits, as anyone with a certain gastrointestinal slowdown can attest.

However, even those praising prune juice's medicinal properties likely don't drink it for pleasure or recreation: It's not known for going down smooth. This makes *prune juice* a perfect term for BS that isn't easily or happily swallowed.

One of the earliest known uses is from a 1904 article in *Life* magazine. This pleasingly alliterative phrase could apply to the balderdash and crapspackle of any era: "forty yards of political prune juice and platitude."

The term was also used by one of the greatest English-language poets, Ezra Pound, in a 1929 letter: "If you agree that there ought to be decent writing, something expressing the man's ideas, not prune juice to suit the pub. taste or your taste, you will have got as far as any 'circle' or 'world' ever has."

Given the anti-Semitism that haunts Pound's legacy, he was somewhat of an expert in prune juice and worse.

psilology

This extremely rare word would probably never have been noticed if it hadn't been used by one of the great poets, Samuel Taylor Coleridge.

In 1834 he coined *psilology,* which he defined as "the love of empty noise." Since this sounds like a serious word for important matters, it's a perfect term for bullshit, especially of the pretentious or pseudophilosophical sort.

Coleridge coined several forms of this word, including a synonym that also referred to empty or shallow theorizing: *psilosophy.* And he coined a word for a type of bullshitter, as seen in this 1816 use: "For the French *Philosophers* we should read *Psilosophers.*" Clearly Coleridge did not have a high opinion of pretentious phonies.

By turning *philosophy* into *psilosophy* and *philosophers* into *psilosophers,* Coleridge was ahead of his time. Altering an established word to shift its meaning is very much in tune with the current era of Internet wordplay, in which a server of marijuana is called a *budtender* and situations with partial or dubious anonymity are called *anonymish.* Coleridge would have been a hit on Twitter.

pucky

Hockey as a term for excrement has no relation to the sport—but *pucky* might. *Green's Dictionary of Slang* suggests that there's a relationship between this term and the size and appearance of a hockey puck, which is somewhat turdlike.

Harlan Ellison used variant spelling *horse puckey* back in 1975, and another use from that year (collected in the *Historical Dictionary of American Slang*) helps define the term: "Legend. Scuttlebutt, you mean. Horse pucky."

Bullpucky is also used, and a 1970 example in *Rolling Stone* makes this euphemism not quite euphemistic: "Bull-fucking puckey."

In the 1980s such diverse sources as the movie *The Bad News Bears* and a *Howard the Duck* comic book included the term. Zoologically and linguistically, pucky knows no bounds.

puffball

This vivid word refers to a type of mushroom: That name fits the fungus' bulbous shape. A puffball is also a bullshitter, especially one full of hot air.

Since at least the mid-1700s *puffball* has referred to people and things that are chock full of a whole lot of nothing.

Oxford English Dictionary examples from the 1800s mention an "empty-pated puff-ball" and "a poisonous puff-ball of pride." A 1955 use takes aim at a particular writer: "Isn't that a small price to pay for Sean's superb deflation of the G. K. Chesterton puffball!" Puffballs are blowhards.

The airy, puffed-up nature of this word makes it a natural for the BS lexicon. This also fits right into the lexicon of insults, thanks to the word *ball*. Slang is full of terms such as *shitball, sleazeball, scuzzball,* and *scumball,* not to mention gentler words such as *goofball.*

Like bags, balls are lexical weapons.

quatsch

This sounds like an abbreviation for the Sasquatch—a mythical creature similar to a yeti. But like such beasts as the Minotaur and the trustworthy cable TV journalist, quatsch is pure baloney.

Quatsch is a German word for bullshit adopted into English since the early 1900s. While not common in English, it can be effective, as seen in this 2002 use from the *Irish Times:* "But his protestations that he only puts body parts on show in the name of education and enlightenment are just so much 'quatsch'."

Translation: "That exhibitionist is full of shit: He can't keep his damn clothes on!"

More often this word has been used as an exclamation, and just like "Bosh!" and "Rot!" it's satisfying to exclaim "Quatsch!" It's probably the only word that can both insult and impress a German friend.

rannygazoo

Some BS words sound very serious, like *sophistry* and *balductum.* Others sound folksy and kinda silly, like *taradiddle* and *rannygazoo.*

This exuberant term with an unknown origin referred to a prank when it started appearing in the late 1800s, and that meaning stuck around. A 1973 use by Spider Robinson in *Analog Science Fiction & Fact* magazine refers to some kind of punking, or at least punching: "Callahan is tolerant of rannygazoo; he maintains that a bar should be 'merry', so long as no bones are broken unintentionally." Today a barkeep might say, "Have fun, but for Christ's sake don't send anyone to the hospital."

Like other types of foolishness, *rannygazoo* shifted to meaning general nonsense. A 1994 use from the *Toronto Sun* mentions the wisdom of avoiding "all that rannygazoo." Like pranks and other BS, rannygazoo is rarely welcome.

I'm not exactly sure what was intended by a 1940 reference in *Time* magazine to a "ring-tailed, rabble-rousing rannygazoo," but it would make a memorable insult or tweet today.

ratchet mouth

A ratchet is a notched wheel, the kind found in many machines: *ratchet* inspired the term *ratchet mouth* for a blabberer. The idea is that just as a ratchet keeps turning noisily, the ratchet mouth keeps chattering noisily. Since the early 1970s a *ratchet jaw* or *ratchet mouth* has been someone who keeps chitchatting, like a ratchet in a factory that just won't stop. If only a ratchet mouth had an off switch.

That led to the term being used for talking nonsense. In George V. Higgins' 1981 novel *The Rat on Fire,* a character says, "I never turn the damned CB on anymore. Too many assholes ratchet-mouthin' shit at each other."

This term has nothing to do with a recent slang meaning of *ratchet* as slutty or skanky. I wager whoever uses that sexist term is just a ratchet mouth in the older sense.

rhubarb

How did the innocent rhubarb make its way from the earth to our plates to the lexicon of bullshit?

Partly due to its sour, bitter taste. That face you make after eating rhubarb sans sugar is likely not that different from the face you make after hearing a heaping helping of hooey.

But there are other reasons *rhubarb* joined the bullshit lexicon. Mainly it was used as background chatter by actors trying to simulate a crowd of people in conversation. These background actors would murmur, "Rhubarb rhubarb rhubarb rhubarb." This 1926 use in the *Manchester Guardian* indicates that this sound effect was performed not only by actors: "If the piece is an elaborately mounted play, requiring a very large mob of people, then everyone in the theatre is pressed into service. . . . The usual murmur of a 'mob' consists of the mysterious word 'rhubarb.'"

Since *rhubarb* was literally a part of meaningless talk, it became a word for meaningless talk. A 1929 use from Iowa's *Rock Valley Bee* makes a timeless statement about a topical subject: "I will tell you what it is, politics. It is rhubarb."

rigmarole

If you've ever had to jump through a bunch of hoops just to do something very simple—like the kind of paperwork parade involved in anything insurance related—you've experienced a rigmarole. This is a term for an annoying bunch of nonsense, which can take a couple of forms.

Rigmarole has a fairly clear origin: It's a variation of *Ragman's roll*. As far back as the 1400s, Ragman was a game in which players pulled objects out of a roll of writing by strings: The object at the end of the string was a surprise. But the *Ragman's roll* or *roll of Ragman* also became a name for a list of any sort before coming to mean, as the *Oxford English Dictionary* puts it, "a long or rambling discourse," also known as a bunch of bloviation.

A use in the *London Times* from 1955 gives a good sense of *rigmarole* as a word for procedural bullshit: "the whole rigmarole of scheduling, listing, and building preservation orders." And a 1964 use from the same paper shows how *rigmarole* applies to lexical bullshit: "The plaintiff was a person given to rigmarole and to wild statements." Whenever wild statements are given, someone's bullshit detector is going beep-beep-beep.

You can also use the adjective *rigmarolic* for lengthy, patience-testing nonsense, and *rigmarolery* is a rare synonym for *rigmarole* itself. An 1839 example from *Blackwood's Edinburgh Magazine* offers a timeless observation: "Sentimental rigmarolery and practical benevolence seldom go together."

rot

I hate to break it to you, but we're all going to rot someday—unless we're cremated. Even then, we're still dead. Death is the ultimate bullshit. Like garbage and caca, the gross reality of rot makes it a fitting term for bushwa.

Rot has been used in English as a BS term since at least the mid-1800s. Two of the greatest English-language playwrights were apparently fond of the term. In 1911's *Fanny's First Play*, George Bernard Shaw wrote, "I quite agree that harlequinades are rot." In 1956's *Long Day's Journey into Night*, Eugene O'Neill wrote, "It's damned rot! I'd like to see anyone influence Edmund more than he wants to be."

Like *bosh* and *paff*, *rot* is most often used as a one-word exclamation. "Rot!" just looks right with an exclamation mark.

rubbish

Rubbish might tie with *nonsense* as the number one synonym for *bullshit*. It's a word with a long history of referring to stuff nobody wants.

Since the 1400s *rubbish* has been used to mean trash, garbage, and refuse of all sorts, including figurative rubbish that offends the brain rather than the nose. Even Shakespeare used a few garbagey terms in *Julius Caesar:* "What trash is Rome? What Rubbish, and what Offall?"

Since at least the 1500s *rubbish* has referred to nonsense or any ridiculous notion. A use in the 1972 second edition of Tim Dinsdale's book *The Loch Ness Monster* offers a plausible explanation for sightings of the legendary monster: "Perhaps it *was* all a lot of rubbish—the misguided chatter of silly people!"

This word is so versatile it can even refer to bullshit created by other species. For example, this 1774 observation: "This robin afterwards sung three parts in four *nightingale;* and the rest of his song was what the bird-catchers call *rubbish,* or no particular note whatsoever." Rubbish is bird bullshit too.

ruck

This word may be out of fashion, but it has a long history in the bullshit lexicon.

In its earliest uses *ruck* referred to something that often comes up when reading about bullshit: a pile or heap. That meaning was broadened when a ruck also came to mean a different kind of heap: a crowd of people.

By the late 1800s this was a word for nonsense. An 1882 article from *Century Magazine* refers to "heterogeneous ruck," which reinforces the pile-of-crap sense. A use in Dow Mossman's 1972 novel *The Stones of Summer* includes another near-synonym for nonsense: "But this is ruck! This is a sophomore's riddle!"

Whether you call it a sophomore's riddle or ruck, it's still bullshit.

sack mouth

Sack gets a lot of mileage in the world of slang. *Sack* refers to the scrotum, and you can also call someone a sack of shit. If you got sacked, you got fired. In the military, sack duty is a nap. To hit the sack with someone is to have sex.

But this term for a gossiper is a bit simpler: A sack mouth is so called because their mouth is like the opening of a sack, especially one that's spilling out everything inside, from last night's dream to last year's vacation. A sack mouth is a blabbermouth.

You can also say someone is *sack mouthing*, a term recorded in Edith A. Folb's 1980 *Runnin' Down Some Lines: The Language and Culture of Black Teenagers*. When you're sack mouthing, you're blathering for the sake of blah-blah.

schm-

Yiddish is full of insulting, humorous words that start with the *schm-* sound, such as *schmuck, schmo,* and *schmaltz,* not to mention the similar-sounding *schlemiel* and *schlimazel*. Thanks to those words and others, the *schm-* sound itself became a suffix with the power to call bullshit on any word or concept.

The earliest known example is from Izak Goller's 1929 novel *The Five Books of Mr. Moses*: "'I know he made Davy go to the Palace to-day with the idea of hastening on the crisis in his illness.' '*Crisis-shmisis!*' mocked Barnett disparagingly." If you search the Internet, you can find this prefix applied to just about everything, including family, schmamily; synergy, schmynergy; president, schmesident; and kale, schmale.

At the risk of blasphemy, here are versions for some of the most popular religious and mythological figures. Warning: Reading the whole list aloud could result in the most coordinated eternal damnation of all time.

God, schmod!
Jesus, schmesus!
Thor, schmor!
Loki, schmoki!
Zeus, schmeus!
Buddha, schmuddha!
Ganesha, schmanesha!
Superman, schmuperman!

Scotch mist

Scotch mist is likely as old as Scotland: It's a thick, wet fog that's common in the Scottish hills. It might be best known from the proverb "A Scotch mist wets an Englishman to the skin." It also can refer to heavy rain.

Scotch mist is a type of bullshit as goopy and blinding as fog. Figurative Scotch mist clouds your mind the way literal Scotch mist clouds the air. In 2014 blogger John Meffen responded skeptically to the notion that Nigeria was Ebola-free: "But that is just a bunch of scotch mist anyway."

The moist, nebulous nature of Scotch mist led to its being used in the sarcastic expression "What do you think that is, Scotch mist?" If you complained that you couldn't find your keys, and I spotted them nearby, I could jerk-ishly say, "What do you think that is, Scotch mist?"

Scotch mist is also a type of whiskey drink—with crushed ice and lemon, served without hooey.

sell wolf tickets

This term has a few meanings related to nonsense—and the closely related genre of boasting.

In *Homicide*—the book that inspired the TV show of the same name—David Simon uses the term, describing a de-fendant "performing in the courtroom, signifying, passing wolf tickets." In this case a wolf ticket is a boast or threat, presumably inspired by the predatory, carnivorous nature of a wolf. The expression "crying wolf" might also be an influence.

To *sell wolf tickets,* then, means to threaten someone or brag about yourself. Think of it as the lexical equivalent of a wolf howl. This sense goes back to around 1969. But in the seventies the term took on a nonsense-related meaning. If you were selling wolf tickets, you were a bullshit merchant. In 1974 journalist Vern E. Smith used the term in his crime novel *The Jones Men,* showcasing a meaning that's very close to BS: "He just stands there sellin' wolf tickets like a God-dam fool." *Selling wolf tickets* can also mean straight-up lying, as seen in a definition from online dictionary *Teen Lingo:* "Trying to get someone to believe a falsity. Spreading lies."

David Simon must love this term, because it also turns

up in *The Wire*, where Major Cedric Daniels defends a theory of Detective Lester Freamon's by saying, "Lester Freamon is not in the habit of selling wolf tickets." On the episode commentary, novelist and episode writer George Pelecanos explained the term: "It means he don't play, he don't lie."

Also, he don't bullshit.

shazbot

Among Robin Williams' first of many contributions to American culture was the goofy alien Mork from Ork. On *Mork & Mindy*, Williams' Mork engaged in many types of odd behavior—such as sitting on his head and drinking from his finger—but one of the most lasting was the use of Orkian obscenities such as *shazbot*.

Shazbot has been around since September 14, 1978, the date of the *Mork & Mindy* pilot. As Mork tries to open his luggage—which is stored in an egg—he says the first *shazbot*. The *sh* sound plus the frustration make it pretty clear this is a euphemism for *shit*. And like *shit, shazbot* grew into and continues to be used as a word for bullshit.

Shazbot isn't commonly used, but it is beloved by many writers on the Internet, particularly geeky writers, such as a member of a gaming forum who wrote, "The game is decent, fine . . . but the company is a load of shazbot." A use in another geek-focused blog mentions a character who "makes up a whole bunch of shazbot." When you're making stuff up, you're solidly in the bullshit zone.

Following the sad death of Robin Williams in 2014, *shazbot* was used as an expression of grief. The word was a perfect way to express shock at his death while honoring Mork's lexical legacy.

shenanigan

This word has an unknown origin but a clear meaning.

Shenanigan—or, more commonly, *shenanigans*—fits in the nonsense/foolishness part of the bullshit spectrum, though the word started in the world of trickery/scams. Shenanigans are full of duplicity and deceit. When the New England Patriots were accused of deflating footballs for an advantage in early 2015, a *Newsday* article used the S-word aptly: "The use of improperly inflated footballs may not have been the only shenanigans employed by the Patriots in last month's AFC Championship Game." Translation: "This team has cheated before, and who knows what else they've been up to?"

Shenanigan as a word has been around since the 1800s, and uses drift between cheating and malarkey. In S. S. Van Dine's 1930 mystery *The Scarab Murder Case,* the word is closer to foolishness: "There's too much shenanigan going on around here to suit me. I want action." In other words, "Cut the bullshit."

shit

Bullshit is one of the most satisfying words in English, but much of that appeal is thanks to its lexical parental unit *shit.*

Before there was *bullshit,* there was *shit.* And in a way, *shit* was always bullshit.

The origins of *shit* are Germanic, but the *Oxford English Dictionary*'s first examples of *shit* in English are not for general poo-poo but for cattle diarrhea.

By the 1500s *shit* was being used as a term for any kind of dung or manure, and also figuratively for an asshole or a son of a bitch. *Shit* took a turn toward bullshit in the 1800s, when it started being used as a synonym for rubbish and other worthless things. An 1890 use from *The Memoirs of Cora Pearl*—"The Government is a load of shit"—could have been written today.

In the twentieth century *shit* started to be used for bullshit's close synonym *nonsense,* as well as for lies and other questionable verbiage. The word has been used by some of English's greatest authors. Aldous Huxley shows his talents extend to shit-slinging in this quotation from a 1930 letter: "In every case something precious and lovely had been taken away and replaced by a mound of shit."

Many *shit* idioms have a meaning on the bullshit spectrum. "Shooting the shit" is often a form of bullshitting. If you don't know shit from shinola, your bullshit detector is faulty.

Often, shit is just bullshit that's more succinct.

shit sandwich

I first learned this term, also known as *praise sandwich,* in graduate school when being taught how to tutor students. I was told to serve them shit sandwiches.

The idea behind *shit sandwich* is that no one likes criticism, so it's best to pack the criticism within soft buns of praise. For example:

Dear Dave,

I appreciate the effort you put into your paper.
That said, your argument is illogical, your sentences are not grammatical, and half of this is plagiarized.
Well, thanks for putting your name on the paper.

Hope this helps,
Professor Peters

The shit sandwich also seems to be used in the business world. A blog post by Walter Chen on managing people is called "The Shit Sandwich and Other Terrible Ways to Give Feedback."

Since the 1960s *shit sandwich* has also been a term for any crappy situation. A common saying is "Life is a shit sandwich. And every day is another bite."

skimble-skamble

The reduplicative word *skimble-skamble* is defined in the ever-dry *Oxford English Dictionary* as "confused, incoherent, nonsensical, rubbishy." It can be used in all sorts of hodge-podge and helter-skelter situations.

This is one of many words first found in Shakespeare. Here it is in *Henry IV, Part I:* "Such a deale of skimble scamble stuffe / As puts me from my faith." In current English that would mean something like, "This is so much crazy bullshit I don't know what to think anymore. I need a drink."

Over two hundred years later, in 1818, a letter by George Gordon Byron shows the term had not been forgotten, at least by lovers of literature: "Did you read his skimble-skamble about [Wordsworth] being at the head of his own profession, in the eyes of those who followed it?"

This is a terrific word for crappy writing: a creative, patterned term for uncreative, jumbled words.

slaver

Like drivel, slaver is spittle, saliva, or anything else dribbling out of someone's mouth. Trust me, slaver can ruin a first date fast (or so I've heard).

The literal meaning goes back to the 1300s, and it took a while for this term to drip down to the language of bullshit. By the 1800s it had started to mimic *drivel*'s figurative sense.

The first recorded use was by poet Samuel Taylor Coleridge in 1825, and it suggests nothing but contempt: "The coward whine and Frenchified Slaver and slang of the other side." Since slang has often been dismissed (accurately) as the language of criminals and youths, it's not surprising to see it lumped in with slaver.

An 1862 use from the *London Times* paints a clear character portrait in one sentence, describing "a modest man, one to whom such slaver must be loathsome." In any century modest folks tend to loathe slaver: Only the immodest love to spew it.

slop, slip-slop, slow-jaw

Slop has referred to all sorts of liquid messes over the years. Eventually it drifted—like other watery words such as *drivel* and *balderdash*—to the lingo of bullshit.

Specifically, slop is the kind of drippiness associated with excess sentimentality. An Ezra Pound letter from 1917 uses the word in that sense, praising writers who "keep out a certain amount of *slop* from the prose section." Great writers never make the reader sleep in the wet spot.

In John Irving's 1978 novel *The World According to Garp,* we see an interesting perspective on journalistic bullshit: " 'Sometimes I feel it is my responsibility to say no,' the editor was quoted as saying, 'even if I know people *do* want to read this slop.' "

In his classic *On the Road,* Jack Kerouac used a variation of *slop:* "Ah, our holy American slop-jaws in Washington are planning further inconveniences." *Slop-jaw* is an exquisite term for a sloppy, prolific bullshitter.

Since *slop* has referred to lousy beer, food, and coffee over the years, it's a natural for bullshit. It's also a natural for reduplication in the form of *slip-slop,* which has been a term for thrown-together drinks, food, and bullshit. When someone you barely know writes a mushy birthday post on your Facebook wall, you couldn't be blamed for responding, "Thanks for the slip-slop!"

small beer

Since the 1400s *small beer* has referred to ales and lagers that are somehow inferior, especially weak beer.

A Shakespeare quote may have paved the way for this term to join the bullshit lexicon, specifically this dismissive, manipulative line from Iago in *Othello* that suggested women are good for nothing except taking care of children and talking about trivialities: "To suckle fooles, and chronicle small Beere." If you're chronicling small beer, you're spinning tales not worth spinning.

By the 1700s *small beer* referred to something close to small potatoes: trivial, insignificant stuff. That puts *small beer* on the trumpery side of the bullshit spectrum. If you think small beer of something, you don't think much of it.

An early 2015 article in the UK's *Essex County Standard* shows the term is not totally out of use: "Ed Balls has dismissed allegations of tax-dodging by Labour as 'small beer', as the bitter row with the Tories over wealthy backers showed no sign of abating."

You can also say a piece of writing is a "small beer chronicle," meaning it's a bunch of trivial twaddle.

sophistry

As the common root indicates, this type of bullshit is one of the most sophisticated.

When you practice sophistry, you're carefully crafting an argument and using the perfect words for your purpose. The only problem is that it's not an honest argument, and you're trying to put one over. Sophistry is high-grade, premium bullshit.

The origins of this word lie with the Greek Sophists. Originally this word had a noble meaning: intellectuals or people devoted to learning. As the reputation of the Sophists declined, a sophist became known not for learning but for creating specious arguments designed to hoodwink. The term *sophistry* has been around since the 1300s, but the practice is likely as old as offers to buy the hills.

Sophistry is on the opposite end of the bullshit spectrum from gibberish. Gibberish might puzzle you, but sophistry could make you buy the wrong house, vote for the wrong candidate, or make a bad decision on a jury. Sophistry uses logic and argumentation to fool you, making it the trickiest bullshit of all.

Gibberish baffles. Sophistry bamboozles.

spin

This mostly political term dates from the 1970s. *Spin* is often described by journalists as either negative or positive. If a congressman gets caught trading government secrets for cash and sex, he'll have to work like a demon to find a positive spin. If his opponent saved orphans from hungry bears, it will take even more work to find a negative spin.

Press agents and other members of a campaign or administration who deal with the media are also called *spin doctors*. This term popped up in the 1980s, and an uncertain (though plausible) explanation for its origin is contained in this 1988 use from Toronto's *Globe & Mail:* "Some of the spin doctors (whose nickname is believed to come from baseball, where pitchers put spin on a ball to control its direction) will be using cellular phones to call in policy specialists."

This kind of professional bullshit artist can also be called a *spin-meister,* although I prefer to think of them as bullshit maestros.

squit

This word could easily be mistaken for *squirt,* and it shares one meaning in common: A squit is a pip-squeak.

Some famous writers have used this word with seeming glee, such as George Bernard Shaw ("Some little squit of a nervous boy") and Aldous Huxley ("Miserable scrofulous little squit!"). Such uses refer to people who lack not only stature but also significance. A squit is a person easily dismissed.

From there the term shifted in meaning from insignificant people to insignificant matters—such as bullshit. This 1893 use by H. T. Cozens-Hardy lumps *squit* with another bullshit word: "Some people may look upon this correspondence as a lot of squit and slaver." In the 1958 play *Roots,* Arnold Wesker uses the word in a very unromantic statement: "Love? I don't believe in any of that squit—we just got married." And a 1976 use from the UK's *Norwich Mercury* offers good advice to us all: "Don't talk squit."

Squit hasn't been very successful, but it probably should be. Any bullshit word that rhymes with *shit* has untapped potential.

straw

It's likely that this term's place in the bullshit lexicon has to do with the weak composition of straw. You can't build a house with straw, and a straw man has no place in a strong argument. Therefore, a bunch of straw is a bushel of horse apples.

This meaning probably evolved from other uses that play on the light, weak nature of straw. Shakespeare used *straw* in this sense in *The Tempest:* "Strongest oathes, are straw / To th' fire ith' blood." Translation: Talk is cheap.

Though it's rare today, *straw* as nonsense is quite old, going back to the 1400s. Just like *bosh, rot,* and *paff,* this was a satisfying word to exclaim after hearing a plethora of palaver.

street yarn, hearsay

The old-fashioned regional term *street yarn* (mostly from New England) is used for the kind of unreliable gossip heard where decent people never go—the streets.

Two examples from the *Dictionary of American Regional English* show the lexical cohorts of this term. An 1850 use in Ohio's *Defense Democrat* mentions "tittle tattle, gossip, street yarn, foolish exagerations [*sic*], scandal, and news mongering." A piece of advice in a column in the *Syracuse (New York) Post Standard* on September 13, 1953, read: "Feathers, fans, dress, sofa-lolling, scandal-making, wearing kids, talking nonsense, and street-yarning do not make the true woman."

A word's company tells you a lot about its meaning, and *street yarn*'s company includes *gossip, nonsense, tattle, news mongering, scandal,* and *foolish.* Not the most respectable bunch.

Street yarn is firmly planted in the gossip region of the bullshit spectrum, and both halves of this term reinforce that meaning. A yarn is rarely reliable: It's a story someone is spinning, and spinning doesn't usually involve telling the plain truth. Meanwhile, the word *street* has plenty of shady associations, often relating to crime and other unsavory activity.

Street yarn is a folksy synonym for a bullshit word often found in legal situations: *hearsay.*

People have been using *hearsay* since the 1500s. In the 1700s examples of *hearsay evidence* started popping up as the legal meaning emerged. These days you don't have to watch a TV lawyer for long before hearing about how something is "just hearsay." As far as the law is concerned, it's a street yarn.

stuff and nonsense

You'll have to go a long way to find a word more general and versatile than *stuff.* Since it was first used as a term for various types of equipment in the 1300s, it's been applied to virtually everything in the world. No wonder it's also used in a bullshit idiom.

Though *stuff and nonsense* has been more successful, *stuff* can mean rubbish all on its own, as seen in a 1701 use by George Farquhar in *Sir Harry Wildair:* "Stuff! stuff! stuff!—I won't believe a Word on't." "Stuff! Stuff! Stuff!" means about the same as "Rot! Bosh! Crap!" Or "Bullshit!"

The usual formula can also be reversed, as in this 1770 use in Samuel Foote's play *The Lame Lover:* "Pshaw! Nonsense and stuff." But the most common idiom puts *stuff* before *nonsense,* as here in Henry Mayhew's 1851 nonfiction book *London Labour and the London Poor:* "It's all stuff and nonsense, all this talk about dust-yards being unhealthy."

This expression is characteristic of the flexibility and creativity of language: Sometimes there's so much nonsense that the word *nonsense* just isn't enough.

stultiloquence

So many BS words are coarse and vulgar. Even the euphemisms, like *horse hockey,* aren't going to go over well with the upper crust of society. The BS lexicon is mostly lower crust.

Then there's *stultiloquence.*

Though this term has a beautiful sound that almost rhymes with *eloquence,* it means the exact opposite: silly bullshit. The roots of *stultiloquence* refer to foolishness and talking—never a great combination. An 1893 use by Algernon Charles Swinburne in *Studies in Prose and Poetry* denounces "the blank and blatant jargon of epic or idyllic stultiloquence." Then as now, writers had pretty strong opinions about writing that sucks.

A quite poetic use in a blog post by James Gleick shows that the word is still in use. Gleick was writing in 2013 about the Library of Congress collecting tweets: "The library will take the bad with the good: the rumors and lies, the prattle, puns, hoots, jeers, bluster, invective, bawdy probes, vile gossip, epigrams, anagrams, quips and jibes, hearsay and tittle-tattle, pleading, chicanery, jabbering, quibbling, block writing and ASCII art, self-promotion and humble-bragging, grandiloquence and stultiloquence."

stump water, stumptalker

The BS term *stump water,* which is mainly used in the south and southern midland of the United States, first came down from the sky.

Stump water was rainwater: specifically, rainwater pooled in a hollow stump. Various ailments, such as warts, were treated with stump water by people who did not have a medical license. Thank goodness no one makes silly, unfounded medical decisions these days!

From there *stump water* became a term for liquor, especially weak liquor. It could also mean weak coffee. Let's face it: If a cup of coffee or glass of booze reminds you of rainwater in a stump, it's bullshit. And *stump water* ended up meaning bullshit too.

This term is mainly used as an exclamation, like "Oh, stump water!" But if someone is stupid, you can also say their head is full of stump water.

This term was used with a variation in a 2014 editorial in the *Crossville (Tennessee) Chronicle,* as Phil Chesser summarized and responded to a letter: "A recent *Chronicle* letter writer objected to our use of the word socialism—he called us Stumptalkers and characterized our columns as stump water—suggesting that our use of the word was not broad enough because it referred only to what he called state socialism."

Stumptalker: a bullshitter more waterlogged than most.

sweet Fanny Adams

Sweet Fanny Adams has been around since at least the 1920s, and it's defined in the 1925 dictionary *Soldier and Sailor Words* as "the polite form of a vulgar phrase." Which phrase? *Sweet fuck-all:* a negating obscenity that means diddly-squat, squadoosh, zilch—in sum, nada. If you have sweet fuck-all, you have nothing.

Naturally *sweet Fanny Adams* has also referred to the fanny, but fortunately for our purposes, it has also referred to nonsense. When the topic is bullshit, an assy term is perfect.

In 1941's *They Die with Their Boots Clean,* Gerald Kersh makes the bullshitty meaning clear: "Never, definitely never, have I heard such a load of Sweet Fanny Adams as

this horrible man comes out with." The formula "load of
_____" tips readers off to the meaning, because nothing is so
commonly measured by the load as bullshit.

This term is closely related to other slangy exclamations
such as the euphemistic "Sweet fancy Moses!" and the not-
so-euphemistic "Sweet bleeding Jesus!"

talk through one's hat

English has more than a millinery shop's worth of hat-
related idioms. Heroes and villains are white hats and black
hats. "I'll eat my hat" is a vivid exaggeration, as in "I'll eat
my hat if tinfoil hats are useful." And if you're talking a lot
of garbage, you're talking through your hat.

One of the earliest uses is an 1888 example from *New
York World*: "Dis is only a bluff dey're makin'—see! Dey're
talkin' tru deir hats."

In any dialect, the hat is a bullshit megaphone.

talk through one's neck

A cruder, and probably more familiar, version of this expression involves talking out of a certain orifice. But I
reckon this folksy expression, due to its absurdity, is even
fitter for bullshit. Since it's impossible to talk through your
neck—ventriloquism and tracheotomies aside—every part
of this expression is suspect.

The oldest known use is from E. W. Hornung's 1899 novel *Amateur Cracksman:* " 'Don't talk through yer neck,' snarled the convict. 'Talk out straight, curse you!' "

You can intensify this expression by accusing someone of talking out the back of their neck. A use in Paul Beatty's 2000 novel *Tuff* pretty much defines itself: "I was talking out the back of my neck and said some shit without really thinking."

targ manure

Star Trek has been kind to the English language, contributing terms such as *cloaking device* and *warp speed* and catchphrases such as "Beam me up, Scotty" and "Damn it, Jim, I'm a doctor, not a . . . "—not to mention the entire Klingon language. But there's also *targ manure,* which is pretty self-explanatory: It's the feces of a targ and a straight-up synonym for BS.

What's a targ? It's a little like a boar but—like most things Klingon—meaner and more dangerous. Also, it has a spiky back.

The term was first used in the 1998 *Star Trek: Voyager* episode "In the Flesh." Here's the conversation between grouchy groundskeeper Mr. Boothby and Lieutenant Commander (and Vulcan) Mr. Tuvok:

BOOTHBY: Targ manure! United Federation of Planets, tolerance for all species, the Prime Directive . . . targ manure, every word of it!

TUVOK: Your metaphor is colorful but inaccurate.

BOOTHBY: Vulcan logic, add that to the list.

Klingons hunt targs for meat, and they also drink their milk. If that's as yucky as it sounds, *targ milk* would also be a solid—er, liquid—term for bullshit.

tomfoolery

Silliness, nonsense, hullabaloo, and ballyhoo are often described as *tomfoolery,* a nineteenth-century word for hijinks.

Why *tom*? Was there a Thomas whose bullshit was so deep it inspired a new word, much as trapeze artist Jules Léotard inspired the word *leotard*?

Nah, *Tommy* was just a name for a simpleton in the 1800s. So a translation of *tomfoolery* would be "idiot bullshit." Or "moron malarkey." Or "dum-dum drivel." You get the idea.

A few variations exist. If you're prone to tomfoolery, you're *tomfoolish*. You can also find an obscene, slangy variation: *tomfuckery*. And a straight-up synonym for *tomfoolery* is *tomfoolishness*, which is used in a sentence from Jerome Klapka Jerome's 1889 novel *Three Men in a Boat*. "Of all the irritating silly tomfoolishness by which we are plagued, this 'weather-forecast' fraud is about the most aggravating."

Tomfoolery is also Cockney rhyming slang for jewelry.

tommyrot

Rot is a longtime member of the BS club, and it has a variation that's also quite successful: *tommyrot*.

Like *tomfoolery*, this word is inspired by the sense of *Tommy* as a word for an idiot. Similar terms that have not been as successful are *thomas rot, tommy nonsense,* and *tommy tripe*.

An 1895 use from the *Chicago Advance* includes an amusing variation: "A whole school of what has been humorously called erotic and tommyrotic realists" who believe "progress in art requires the elimination of moral ideas."

Also, a *tommyrotter* is a con man.

trash talk

In the Venn diagram of bullshit and boasting, there's a landfill of trash talk.

Though *trash talk* is a perfect synonym for *rubbish,* it has a more specific meaning: boasting about yourself and belittling others. Sports are the most fertile ground for trash talk: Players love to talk shit.

Though this is a sports term, it's also used widely in situations not involving running or balls. A *Time* article from 2002 described a Supreme Court decision with language you'd expect from Marv Albert: "The dissenters concluded that the majority had 'acted unwisely'—which passes for serious trash talk on the high court."

Speaking of courts, Michael Jordan and Charles Barkley were not only two of the best basketball players of all time but also hall-of-fame trash-talkers. Barkley has had this to say about the art of trash talk: "These kids today think trash-talking means getting real personal and challenging your manhood. They're missing the point. It's just about trying to get to the other guy a little bit, having fun."

Barkley's point: Don't take trash talk too seriously. It's just a bunch of garbage.

treacle

Some bullshit is sneaky. Other bullshit is incomprehensible. This is a type that's sickeningly sweet.

Treacle originally meant a type of medicinal compound, but the meaning that's more relevant evolved in the late 1600s: a type of syrup. Like most syrup, treacle was ultra-sweet. And that excess of sweetness allowed *treacle* to seep into the bullshit lexicon.

The main problem with treacle is that it's phony—or at least feels phony. That phoniness is implied in this early 2015 *Ithaca Journal* review of *American Sniper:* "At the 11th hour, for the first time, it devolves into less-than-credible treacle. Maybe it's true that in the final few moments that Kyle's wife ever spent with her doomed husband, she did indeed give him a saccharine speech about how glad she was that he'd recovered from his PTSD, come back to his family and made them proud—but it sure feels more like a Hollywood ending than real life."

The phrase "saccharine speech" is fitting. Treacle is an extremely artificial sweetener.

tripe

Of all the vile, disgusting, grody words in the bullshit lexicon, this might be the grossest.

The first meaning, circa 1300, is described by the *Oxford English Dictionary* as "the first or second stomach of a ruminant, esp. of the ox, prepared as food; formerly including the entrails of swine and fish." The term has also been used for the guts of any animal, including people. No wonder this became a word for being full of it: We are all literally full of tripe. Fittingly, "bag of tripe" also became an insult.

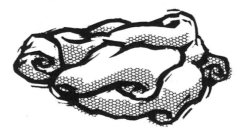

Tripe took on a rubbishy meaning in the 1700s that has continued today. A 1927 book called *Romantic Friendship* offered this observation: "Ordinary talk is such ghastly tripe once voice and gesture are removed."

Given its gut-centric origin, this is a word best used for the bullshit that makes you sick to your stomach.

There's also a variation that's kind of related to bullshit: A *tripe-hound* is a reporter or informant.

truck

Given that *load* is such a BS-friendly word, it shouldn't be surprising that *truck* has also hauled some lexical refuse.

A 1913 use from Jack London's novel *The Valley of the Moon* conveys the shift from *stuff* to *bullshit:* "Talk about pluggin' away at a job in the city, an' goin' to movin' pictures and Sunday picnics for amusement! . . . I can't see what was eatin' me that I ever put up with such truck." And Mark Twain used the term in an 1866 letter: "You can go on writing that slop about balmy breezes and fragrant flowers, and all that sort of truck."

Sadly, we all put up with a lot of truck. Sometimes life is a truckload of truck.

trumpery

Here's a BS word with a long history and many specific purposes, tiny and tricky though they may be.

The first was a type of hornswoggling. Trumpery was originally practiced by criminals and scam artists. Like so many other words related to trickery and bridge selling, the word shifted to mean more general nonsense, this one in the 1400s. *Oxford English Dictionary* examples often involve something mystical or woo-woo: There's a mention of "metaphysical trumpery," and superstition and Freemasonry both get lumped with trumpery. A Ouija board is a good example of trumpery.

Insignificance is also key to trumpery. If something matters at all, it can't be trumpery. Internet outrage is a good example of trumpery: If someone is treating a magazine cover (featuring, say, airbrushing or breast-feeding) as though it were the second coming of Stalin, that's trumpery: a trumped-up triviality.

A 2013 review of the movie *Adore* in the *San Francisco Chronicle* embraces the distracting, unwanted essence of *trumpery:* "There's so much trumpery on parade, including a relentless air of self-importance, that it's even hard to simply enjoy the performances of the two stars, who give more than the film deserves." Sounds like it could have been a good movie if not for the pretentious BS.

truthiness

The Colbert Report, which ran from 2005 to 2014, was a remarkable show. Stephen Colbert's puffed-up, preposterous satire of right-wing cable blowhards who wrap themselves in too many flags and not enough facts was one of the smartest, funniest shows in the history of television. Every episode, nearly every joke, exposed bullshit. So it's fitting that in the very first episode Colbert coined a new word that has, so far, been the most successful new BS term of the twenty-first century.

It debuted in what would go on to be a very popular segment: "The Word." As *truthiness* appeared next to him, Colbert pontificated: "Now I'm sure some of the word police, the wordinistas over at *Webster's*, are gonna say, 'Hey, that's not a word.' Well, anybody who knows me knows that I'm no fan of dictionaries or reference books. They're elitist. Constantly telling us what is or isn't true, or what did or didn't happen. Who's *Britannica* to tell me the Panama Canal was finished in 1914? If I want to say it happened in 1941, that's my right. I don't trust books. They're all fact, no heart." Colbert, on the other hand, was all heart and no brains with this vow: "The truthiness is anyone can read the news to you. I promise to feel the news at you." *Truthiness* ended up being selected as the American Dialect Society's Word of the Year for 2005.

Though Colbert made up *truthiness,* he wasn't the first do so. In fact, there's an example of *truthiness* in the *Oxford English Dictionary* from 1824: "Everyone who knows her is aware of her truthiness." That meaning was the opposite of Colbert's: full of truth rather than lacking it.

Five years after the birth of *truthiness,* Colbert revealed its origin story to lexicographer Ben Zimmer in an interview for *Visual Thesaurus,* saying he was looking for a word that embodied "feelings rather than thought." Also, Colbert said, "I wanted a silly word that would feel wrong in your mouth." He almost went with plain old *truth* but followed this train of thought: "Well, it's not truth. It's *like* truth. It's truth*ish*. It's truth*y*. But I needed a noun. So I said, 'It's truth*iness*.'"

Colbert didn't just launch a new word for bullshit: He added a new suffix to the language or, rather, changed the meaning of an existing suffix to reflect a new meaning. Due to the success of *truthiness*, other writers started using *-iness* to coin words that had a bullshit flavor. The Colbert suffix—so named by linguist Arnold Zwicky—disparaged concepts much like the *schm-* prefix.

Examples include *democraciness, doubtiness, factiness, fame-iness, referenciness, scienciness,* and *youthiness.* The Colbert suffix was also part of at least one book title: Charles Seife's *Proofiness: How You're Being Fooled by the Numbers.*

twaddle, twittle-twattle

Twaddle, which started appearing in the 1700s, is likely a variation of *twattle,* an older word with a similar meaning. Other words in the *twaddle* family tree include *tittle* (to whisper) and *tattle* (to snitch or rat).

Twaddle shares a sound with *Twitter* and *tweet,* and it shares qualities with this popular social network. Long before people wrote in 140 characters or less, twaddle was writing and talking that was silly, insignificant, clichéd, or just pretentious. *Twaddle* was a versatile word that could mean anything from small talk to painful academese. There are also some amusing variations, such as *twaddledom, twaddlize,* and *twaddlesome.*

Though it's a little old-fashioned, *twaddle* has never gone completely out of style. In early 2015, Liam Reddington of the Plain English Campaign used *twaddle* alongside some of its synonyms in a memorable denouncement of a letter by Dundee City Council education director Michael Wood: "The message is lost in a deluge of jargon and gobbledegook and therefore the writing is not fit for purpose. It is tripe dissolved in twaddle."

There's also the variation *twittle-twattle,* which has been around since the 1950s.

Twittle-twattle is the hearsay, blabbering type of bullshit. The word is similar in sound and form to several other bullshit words, such as *chitter-chatter, prattle-prattle,* and *tittle-tattle.*

waffle

Someone who is waffling keeps changing their mind—to an annoying degree. If you want to go to the movies, but then you're not sure, and then you say yes, and then maybe, that's waffling. Failure to pick a specific movie could involve a whole new round of waffling. That kind of bullshit is likely why *waffle* is in the BS lexicon.

But how did *waffle* migrate from the breakfast table to the bull session? Are waffles really so fickle and/or full of it?

Nah. This term has a totally different origin that's unrelated to food: *Waffle* was a word for yapping, as in the noises that come out of a tiny dog. That sense apparently led to the word's shifting to cover one of humanity's most annoying noises: gossip. And then it was a small step toward, as the *Oxford English Dictionary* puts it, "verbose but inconsequential talk or writing; empty verbiage."

This twentieth-century term is used characteristically in a 1957 article from the *Economist:* "His ability to distinguish the essence and to cut the waffle in any discussion are [*sic*] exceptional."

"Cut the waffle" is a hell of a way to say "skip the bull-shit." And it's not nearly as easy to do when speaking or writing as it is when making breakfast.

Welshman's hose

Get your mind out of the gutter: It's not that kind of hose.

Rather, this term came about due to a property of hoses we can still see today: They can be stretched out to great lengths. When you combine the word *hose* with a slur against Welshmen—who have always gotten a hard time from the British—you get a term that involves the stretching of the truth. That often produces bullshit.

This expression was commonly found in the phrase "to make a Welshman's hose" of something. This kind of bullshit involved a self-serving interpretation. The earliest known use is from John Skelton's *Here After Foloweth a Litel Boke Called Colyn Cloute* in 1529: "A thousand thousande other / That . . . make a walshmans hose / Of the texte and of the glose." Then and now, a circuitous or pretentious interpretation turns any text into a chaotic, jumbled mess.

Perhaps due to the arbitrary and mean slur against the Welsh, this term is now rare and could use an update. I suggest replacing the innocent Welshman with an annoying douchebag, pretentious hipster, or belligerent blogger.

yakety-yak

Since *yack* (or *yak*) is a word for talking, it's natural that *yakety-yak* would emerge as a term for too much talking. The word is literally talking times two.

The *Oxford English Dictionary*'s earliest examples are, unfortunately, extremely sexist, mentioning "girlish yakitty-yak" and "yackety-yacketing women," not to mention this 1958 use from the *London Observer:* "A muddle-headed momma . . . who knows no better than to drive away her husband . . . by constant yackety-yack and pleas to stay at home."

These uses probably gravitated toward women because *yakety-yak* referred mainly to the gossipy sort of bullshit, and women definitely, totally gossip more than men. At least that's what my buddy Shane heard from his pal Jason.

Those examples were all from the 1950s—a far more sexist age. These days most people are aware that men are quite capable of yakety-yakking with the best of 'em—especially the mansplainers.

yada yada

Blah blah . . . Yada yada . . . Both can be a form of bullshit.

Most people were introduced to this term through *Seinfeld,* specifically "The Yada Yada," an episode from 1997. George initially enjoys his new girlfriend Marcy's use of *yada yada,* thinking her direct and concise when she uses it to omit seemingly irrelevant details. Then he has cause to question the term when Marcy says, "Speaking of exes, my old boyfriend came over late last night, and yada yada yada. Anyway, I'm really tired today."

Much like Stephen Colbert's *truthiness, yada yada* was only spread by *Seinfeld,* not coined on the show. The first known use was by comedian Lenny Bruce, who employed several variations—such as *yahdeyadedah* and *yaddeyahdah*—in a script collected in *The Essential Lenny Bruce.* The word is mainly used by a prisoner named Dutch who has taken some guards hostage. Dutch uses the word to mock the warden's attempts at negotiation.

Since the details replaced by *yada yada* are supposed to be trivial and meaningless, *yada yada* itself came to mean trivial nonsense. In this 2005 use from the *Hoosier Times,* it refers to a common form of bullshit: "The EULA, or 'End-User License Agreement,' is the yada yada yada that you agree to when you install software on your computer. It's usually pages and pages of stuff that no one reads."

Yada yada is often spelled *yadda yadda,* and it has sometimes been spelled *yatta yatta,* with variations such as *yattata-yattata* and *yaddega-yaddega.*

You can also spell it BS.

yammer

Originally this word had a meaning far sadder than bullshit: It referred to lamentations, wailing, whining, and crying. That sense is found as far back as the 1400s. A sad person who suffered many misfortunes was likely to yammer.

Since whining gets old quickly for anyone in earshot, the word shifted in meaning to take on a negative sense. Yammering was no longer just lamenting: It was too much lamenting. Then it was just too much talking, period.

The essence of many bullshit words involves some sort of animal reference, and this word has also shifted in that direction. In Will Henry's *The Seven Men at Mimbres Springs,* published in 1958, the author writes: "Somewhere off in the eastern hills a coyote yammered with the crazed wildness which never fails to startle the oldest listener." Based on that description, yammering coyotes sound a lot more entertaining than their two-legged counterparts.

Acknowledgments

Thanks to my editor, Amanda Patten, for making the book process super smooth. She and everyone else at Penguin Random House (including Robert Siek, Tal Goretsky, Elina Nudelman, Tricia Boczkowski, and Jenni Zellner) were supportive at every turn with never a trace of BS.

Thanks to my agent, Sorche Fairbank, for landing this book deal and making me feel like a big deal. She is a book superhero. I'm pretty sure she was bitten by a radioactive book. Thanks also to Matthew Frederick at Fairbank Literary.

Thanks to Drew Dernavich for collaborating with me and introducing me to Sorche. This book would not have happened without him. Also, his cartoons are freakin' wonderful.

I couldn't have written this book without access to the great digital dictionaries, so thanks to Alice Northover of Oxford University Press, Joan Hall of the *Dictionary of American Regional English,* Jonathon Green of *Green's Dictionary of Slang,* and Kory Stamper of *Merriam-Webster.* Additional thanks for specific advice or general awesomeness to Michael Adams, David Barnhart, Grant Barrett, Erin McKean, and Jesse Sheidlower. You've all made me feel welcome in the word-nerd world.

Thanks to various editors who have published me over the years, but especially Ben Zimmer at *Visual Thesaurus,* David Haglund and Dan Kois at *Slate,* Christopher Monks and John Warner at *McSweeney's,* Adrienne Crezo at *Mental Floss,* Erin Brenner at *Copyediting,* John Holl at *All About Beer,* and Claudia Kawczynska at *The Bark,* where I have the unique title of Comic Book Editor-at-Large.

Most of all, I'd like to thank my parents, Edward and Janet, and also my dog, Monkey, who can read, I think.

About the Author

MARK PETERS is a humorist and journalist. The humor consists of comedy sketches, humor pieces, Twitter jokes (@wordlust, @cnnyourmom, @tswiftnews666), and a cartoon collaboration with Shane Swinnea called *Nachos . . . From The Abyss* (nachoabyss.com). The journalism is about comic books, TV, comedy, dogs, craft beer, and—as you may have guessed from this book—language. Mark lives in Chicago with his dog (a rat terrier named Monkey) and your mom.